Coordinate Movement

for Pianists

Anatomy, Technique, and Wellness Principles

Coordinate Movement
for Pianists

Anatomy, Technique, and Wellness Principles

Lisa Marsh

GIA Publications
Chicago

Coordinate Movement for Pianists

Lisa Marsh

Layout and Design by Martha Chlipala
Edited by Bryan Gibson

Artwork: Figures 4.1, 6.1, 7.1, 7.2, 11.1, 27.1 by Holly Fischer, © Andover Educators, used with permission; Figures 6.2, 7.3, 7.4, 9.1, 9.2, 11.2, 11.3, 11.4, 11.5, 14.1, 26.1, 27.2 by Amanda Rice, used with permission; Figure 13.1 by Ellen Blazich, used with permission.

Cover art: Photograph by Brian Marsh.

G-9987
ISBN: 978-1-62277-398-5

Table of Contents

Part III: Wellness Principles

Preface

This book was originally conceived as a course manual for the Coordinate Movement Master Class at Portland State University. My hope is that the reader will gain new insight into the art and science of piano playing from the topics presented and from the graphics and musical examples that supplement the text.

Acknowledgments

I would like to thank Barbara Conable for her many years of generous teaching and mentoring in the fields of Body Mapping and the Alexander Technique. Her knowledge and pedagogical approach transformed my method of working with musicians.

I am also very grateful for the instruction I received at the Taubman Institute and for the many teachers who inspired me while I was there: Dorothy Taubman, Edna Golandsky, Robert Durso, Kendall Feeney, Nina Scolnik, John Bloomfield, Mary Moran, and Marc Steiner.

Many thanks to my piano technician, Linda Scott, for her insightful additions to the Piano Map chapter.

The information on octaves presented by Thomas Mark for the Coordinate Movement class is the basis for my chapter on octaves and chords. I thank him for his articulate and clear voice.

I also want to thank Mary Kogen for traveling with me to study the Taubman Approach and for being a supreme model of teacher as learner.

My friend Mary Straub spent countless hours reviewing and editing my drafts. I am very grateful for her generous knowledge and support.

My dear friend, author Scott Teitsworth, also provided valuable and graceful editorial comments while encouraging me to finish this book. Thank you, Scott, for your generous spirit.

Thank you to Dr. Marshall Chasin for reviewing the chapter on hearing loss prevention and for helping musicians around the world protect their hearing.

Thank you to Dr. T. Richard Nichols for his valuable additions the chapter on performance anxiety.

To my mentor, Harold Gray, I give profound thanks for believing in me and in the future of piano technique. He is the one who encouraged me to pursue my path of finding ways to help musicians play without pain or injury.

My beautiful daughters, Jennifer, Terra, and Elise, have encouraged me to be a writer, musician, and a mom. Without their support I could not have written this book.

Finally and most importantly, I dedicate this book to my husband, Brian, whose patient kindness has allowed me space in my life to express my true self.

Part I
Anatomy for Pianists

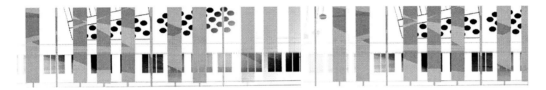

Chapter 1
Sound Equals Movement

To begin the study of piano technique and artistry, it is necessary to define sound and understand how to produce it. For centuries piano studies have been primarily based on the critical interpretive elements with cursory attention given to specific body parts and movements that aid execution. By beginning with a simple equation, sound equals movement, we can proceed from a foundation that allows equal attention to the score and to the human mind and body. Certainly, it is the movement of our bodies that translates the score into sound.

When we study a piece, we develop an aural imagination of how the piece should sound. That is to say we hear the piece in our brain, hopefully in a manner that portrays our ultimate desired sound to some degree. This aural imagination is based on our hearing of the piece from playing through, listening to recordings, and attending live performances. To enhance aural imagination in a thoughtful way, one can consult source references and recordings pertaining to the historical period and composer. By seeking the true intention and playing style of each composer, we can be confident that our aural imagination will be more in sync with the composer's.

Next we must find the movements that will create the imagined sound. The greater the understanding of the structure and function of the body as it relates to sound production, the larger the repertoire of movements available. Coupled with understanding of related anatomy must come a sensory awareness of the nature and quality of each movement. Movements free of unnecessary tension are the most easily controlled and produce the most varied and resonant sound.

As we discover coordinated, free movements in our exploration of a piece, we begin to repeat and reinforce those movements that produce the desired sound. By listening carefully, recording oneself, and accepting guidance from a respected teacher or colleague, we can sort out the actual sound we produce at any moment from the desired sound we have in our heads. Ask yourself: Am I hearing the actual sound I am making, or am I hearing the sound I want to make? In summary, one definition of practicing would include the following three steps: aural imagination, discovering movements that create the desired sound, and repetition of those specific movements.

Ideally, the complexity of the music should be matched by the complexity of the movement. Often this movement is invisible to the observer and can be termed "micro-movement." Thus, famous pianists such as Arthur Rubinstein who appear not to move much actually have many micro-movements throughout their body as they play. Any part of the body that is fixed and prevented from moving interrupts the flow of the music and can lead to injury. Pianists have their own repertoire and scope of movement that makes them unique and portrays their individual artistry.

It is important to sort out the two types of movement used at the piano. The first type includes those movements directly related to sound production, and the second type includes those movements we make in response to the music. Thus, a rotation of the forearm used to play a trill would be category one, and a facial expression would be category two. Both types of movement are valid and necessary. However, the movements in the second category, those made in response to the music, should never undermine those movements specific to sound production. Sometimes pianists with dramatic, large body movements have difficulty controlling the quality and nuance of their sound. Be aware of these different types of movement as you play, and view yourself on a video recording often to sort this out.

A pianist can gain the habit of being aware of the relationship between sound and movement in practice and in performance. By continually evaluating the sounds produced from a movement perspective, powerful tools for controlling and varying the sound are developed.

Chapter 2
Sensory Awareness at the Piano

As pianists, we use four primary senses when we practice and perform. They are the visual, aural, tactile, and kinesthetic senses. We receive information from receptors in our body related to each of these senses that is communicated via the sensory nerves to our brain. The visual sense has receptors in the eye, the auditory sense in the ear, the tactile sense in the skin and lining of the mouth and nasal passages, and the kinesthetic sense has receptors in joints and muscles.

Oddly enough, many pianists are ignorant of the existence of the kinesthetic sense. We are not taught about this sense, and it is often not even named unless you have taken an anatomy or physiology class. The word *kinesthesia* comes from the Greek root *kinein*, to move. The ending *-esthesia* means pertaining to mental responsiveness or awareness. A good working definition of *kinesthesia* for pianists is: the sense that detects bodily position, weight, and tension or movement of the muscles, tendons, and joints. Obviously, sensory information coming to the brain from this sense is of paramount importance if we are working from the foundational principle that sound equals movement.

It is unfortunate that many pianists only become aware of their bodies when strained tendons, muscles, and joints give feedback about inflammation and pain. If we are aware of the nature and quality of our movement at all times as we play, we can avoid misuse and modify our movements when necessary. The cycle of injury often begins with tension and fatigue. If these early warning signs are ignored, inflammation and pain may ensue. Those pianists who push through pain, ignoring it or mistakenly approaching the art of piano playing as a physical test of strength and endurance, may end up with permanent injury.

To fully understand and utilize the kinesthetic sense, it is necessary to have a working knowledge of anatomy pertaining to movement at the piano. Not only must we understand where the movement is coming from, but also what the quality and size of each movement is. For instance, a movement of the left forearm toward the bass register to play a bass note in a waltz figure must be smooth, mostly horizontal, and ideally produced from the shoulder or second arm joint in a "windshield-wiper" fashion.

Throughout this book I will endeavor to be as specific as possible about the location, size, quality, and combination of movements necessary for a fluid piano technique. Your increasing awareness of the movement of your joints, muscles, and tendons in all activities will serve to improve your awareness at the piano.

The tactile sense is less mysterious, as many of us have been taught to "feel our fingers." However, this sense has a depth and richness often overlooked. Sometimes the tactile sense is bundled with the kinesthetic sense, even though they have clearly different receptors in our bodies. Often the tactile and kinesthetic senses do work together, as in the following examples regarding the tactile sense of various parts of the key. It is important to distinguish between the two senses even when they are operating in concert.

When exploring the tactile sense, it is necessary to sort out the various parts of the key and its depth that you are experiencing at any one time. The sense of the top of the key assures proper finger placement on the key. This includes being on the right key and being on the part of the key that is best suited to the notes before and after it. The sense of the key descending includes the kinesthetic sense and relates to dynamics. We shall explore this concept in more depth in Part II, but for now just be aware that the faster the key descent, the louder the sound. Also, feeling the quality of the tactile sense on the keybed, or bottom of the keys, prevents unnecessary pressure at the end of the keystroke. Ideally, the fingers should be rested on the keybed and rebounding easily from key to key. This sensation is not unlike walking across the floor. Just as we do not exert unnecessary pressure with each step, neither do we press on the bottom of the keys. Extra effort on the bottom of the key can lead to strain of the tendons and muscles of the hand and forearm, as well as prevent rebound from one key to the next. Awareness of the feeling of the release of the key utilizes tactile and kinesthetic senses and relates to articulation—the characteristics of attack and decay of single notes or groups of notes. The quicker the release is, the shorter the articulation will be. Thus, staccato sounds require a quick rebound off the bottom of the key and a quick release of the key. Legato sounds require a slower release timed with the depression of the following key. Of course, the pedal aids in producing legato sounds. Many pianists have imagined the depth to the keybed as much greater than it is and need to use their eyes to help them correct that impression.

The aural or auditory sense is probably the most well known to pianists. It is through our listening that we guide our movements to produce the sounds we desire. The auditory and kinesthetic senses must work together.

Our visual sense can be very dominant. It is helpful to play some with your eyes closed to reduce the dominant, sometimes judgmental effect of the visual sense. If you are watching your hands as you play, notice which hand you watch more. Ideally, your visual sense should be balanced between the hands, depending upon where it can best support the other senses. An example of this would be looking ahead to the treble region for a quick leap the right hand needs to make. If you are using your visual sense to read the music, pay attention to the quality of your gaze. Be sure you have adequate light and glasses, if needed, appropriate for the distance of the music.

Included in sensory awareness is our breathing. Tactile receptors in the lining of our nose give us information about the temperature and humidity of the air we breathe. We can feel the movements of breathing with our kinesthetic sense: the outward excursion of our ribs, the expansion of our abdomen and gathering of our spine as we inhale, and the inward excursion of our ribs, the rebound of our abdominal wall, and the lengthening of our spine as we exhale. We will explore these movements more in Chapter 7. By turning our attention to breathing, we allow this life-giving process to operate more freely and effectively. Brain cells receive more oxygen, enhancing mental acuity. Muscles receive the necessary oxygen to keep them free of fatigue and tension. Slow, deep breathing can regulate our heart rate and this can reverse the effects of too much adrenaline in practicing and performing. Attention to breathing supports phrase direction and keeps the music alive and flowing. Above all, sensory awareness of breathing helps us stay embodied and in the present moment—two requirements of healthy artistry.

Sensory awareness can become a way of life. Receiving information from our senses about the world around us supports our presence in the moment. This keeps us connected to our bodies and integrated with all that is happening around us. It is through sensory awareness that musicians acquire the skill of communicating ideas and emotions via music.

Chapter 3
Inclusive Awareness

nclusive awareness is a term borrowed from the Alexander Technique that refers to a type of mindfulness that allows for all the elements of a given subject to be present simultaneously. It mirrors the way our brain functions and is demonstrated in many daily activities, such as driving. Imagine driving a car safely without awareness of the speedometer, the road, the surrounding traffic, and traffic signs. Inclusive awareness is not concentration. Concentration requires paying attention to only one thing to the exclusion of all others. This would be disastrous for a pianist! How could we possibly move all ten fingers, utilize both feet on the pedals, and produce a beautiful sound if we were concentrating on one thing—such as playing the right notes? The concept of inclusive awareness is particularly beneficial to musicians as they practice and perform. With a fluid, broad awareness, musicians can entertain all aspects of music making and brighten certain areas as needed.

Figure 3.1 itemizes some of the components of inclusive awareness necessary for pianists. Notice the three broad categories delineated in this diagram. The first category, embodiment, contains elements of our physical being we need to be aware of as we play. Included are: sensory awareness, breathing, sitting balance, neck muscles, spinal movement, and emotion. The second category contains items external to our physical being that contribute to our sound production: the piano, the room we are playing in, the audience. The third category contains some of the elements of the music itself: the composer, the score, rhythm, dynamics, phrasing, harmony, articulation, tempo, and tone.

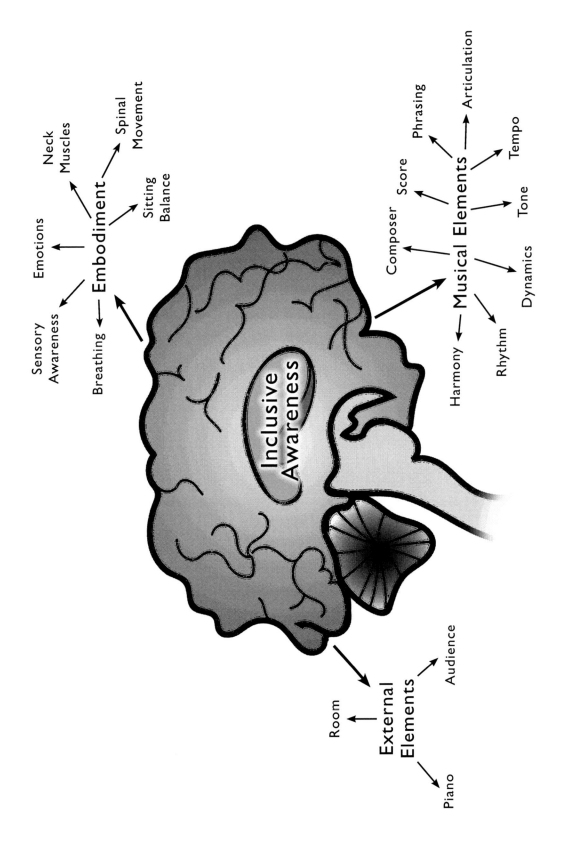

Figure 3.1. Mind Map for Musicians.

At any one time several of these components need to be present in our awareness when we practice or perform. Those elements needed at any one time naturally come to the foreground. For instance, if you were playing from memory and had a memory slip, your knowledge of the harmonic structure could be brightened to find your way back. As you begin to develop an inclusive awareness at the piano, you can enhance the expansion of your mind by practicing inclusive awareness in daily life.

One way to introduce inclusive awareness into your practicing is to layer experiences in your warm-up. Start with a simple experience, such as breathing, and play your first scale with breathing bright in your awareness. Add another element of your experience, such as tone, for the next scale, keeping breathing also in your awareness. Continue layering and keep your mind open to each previous subject.

Inclusive awareness affords a fluid consciousness that is free of tension. When our minds are free of tension, our bodies are less likely to respond in a fixed or tense manner. Some pianists find the concept of inclusive awareness frightening. They believe that they will forget the notes if they do not concentrate on playing the right notes all of the time. However, this is not true. Inclusive awareness allows the pianist to entertain every aspect of music making needed at any given time. Most pianists find it enriching and comforting, almost like finding a more natural, familiar way to approach the instrument.

Chapter 4
Sitting at Balance

To understand sitting at balance, it is necessary to understand the functions of the skeletal and muscular systems. Two of the primary functions of the skeletal system are to support the weight of your body and to deliver that weight into the bench and floor. Muscles are for moving, primarily. If you use your muscles to hold you upright, you will cause unnecessary tension and reduce the facility of movement.

To more fully understand sitting at balance, refine your body map using Figure 4.1. Body maps are the internal representations in our brains of the structure, function, and size of various parts of our bodies. Neuroscientists have explored body maps for decades, and more recently Barbara and William Conable have incorporated body maps into music. This field of somatic education is called "Body Mapping." Through Body Mapping musicians learn to play with more ease and artistry using anatomical information to correct their body maps. Our body maps govern our movement, thus having an adequate and accurate body map is essential for musicians.

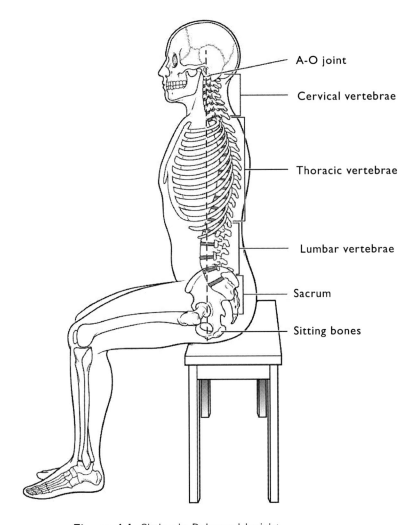

A-O joint

Cervical vertebrae

Thoracic vertebrae

Lumbar vertebrae

Sacrum

Sitting bones

Figure 4.1. Sitting in Balance Upright.

The spine is thickest in the front, so when you sit, the front of your spine receives the weight of your body. Be certain that you have not mapped your spine as straight or too small. When you find the place of balance while sitting, realize that it is a neutral place, not a position. It is not necessary to hold or fix yourself in this place. Rather, consider sitting at balance as a place from where the greatest variety and ease of movement are possible. Now let's look at balance points of the skeletal system in more detail.

The first point is the atlanto-occipital (AO) joint, where the base of the skull meets the first cervical vertebra—the part of your spine in the neck region. When the head is balanced at this joint, there is no tension in the neck or scrunching of the cervical vertebrae. The ears are in line with the shoulders and the eyes gaze at the horizon. There are many kinesthetic receptors in the AO joint. You can feel when your head is balanced by accessing this joint in your sensory awareness. It is located right between your ears and is the midpoint of your skull from front to back and side to side. Many pianists mistakenly create a head/neck unit which moves in front of the torso like a turtle. This misunderstanding, or mismapping, greatly reduces the fluidity of the arm movements due to tension in the neck and trapezius muscle. If you wish to look down at the keys, move from the AO joint and let the spine follow in sequence. You can also just gently tilt your head down from this joint without jutting your head forward.

The second balance point is the arm structure, which we shall explore in great detail in the chapter titled "The Whole Arm." For now be aware of the suspension of your arm structure above the ribs and the position of your shoulder joints in line with your ears. You don't need to hold your shoulders back to sit at balance. Instead, feel your back as open and wide.

The lumbar balance point is next, and it should be directly below the AO joint. Notice how the curve of the spine allows for this relationship. Many people overarch their lumbar spine and end up with low back pain. Explore the range of movement at this balance point by arching your back and then moving through neutral to curve your back. When sitting at balance, the lumbar region is neither arched nor curved. That said, when we play the piano there is a lot of movement which takes us through neutral to an arched or curved position, depending on the passage. Balance is not a position—just a place of no muscular work that affords the greatest variety of movement.

If you do experience back pain while practicing, try the "organist's stretch." Barbara Conable taught this to me and it has helped many pianists. Stretch your arms out to your sides and lean toward the music rack, moving from the hip joint.

Then let your arms float out sideways and hug the ends of the piano. Turn your head to one side as you rest against the front of the piano. Breathe deeply and feel the opening and releasing of the muscles in your back. Then turn your head to the other side and repeat. Let your arms drift back to your sides and slowly sit upright. If turning your head to the side is uncomfortable, rest your forehead on the front of the piano.

When sitting, the sitting bones are the next place of balance and weight delivery. The weight of the head and torso is delivered through the arch of the pelvis into the bench. Notice the rockers, those bones at the base of the pelvis shaped like the bottom of a rocking chair. They contact the bench, delivering your weight and also allowing for a large variety of movement. You can shift your weight forward and back, as in the "organist's stretch," or from side to side.

The weight of the legs is transferred to the floor through the knee and ankle joints. This is a dynamic weight transfer, as your legs move to contact the floor in various places. Awareness of your feet on the floor affords more movement, gives a sense of being centered or grounded, and can also help solidify your internal sense of rhythm. Imagine dancing without feeling your feet on the floor! As you gain more awareness of your legs while playing, pay attention to the quality of the leg muscles. Are you holding your legs together and creating tension in your thighs that travels up to your back? There is no need to hold your legs in any position.

While playing the piano we have three solid surfaces we move in relation to. They are the keybed, which we contact with our fingertips; the bench, which we contact with our rockers; and the floor, which we contact with our feet. Because our bodies are continually in motion, it is important to feel these solid surfaces to avoid creating fixtures in our body. Feeling the bottom of each key gives us a surface from which to rebound to the next note. It is not necessary to put pressure on the keybed. Simply rest there as you would rest the weight of your body on the ground when standing or walking. As mentioned previously, the contact of the rockers with the bench affords movement in all directions with the aid of your feet. The contact of the feet on the floor delivers the weight of the legs into the floor and allows us to move from side to side. Try pushing off with your left foot on the floor—it moves your whole torso to the right! Even the right foot, when resting on the pedal, can help move the torso to the left using your heel.

It is important to mention a serious mismapping concerning the term "waist." Pianists who think of their waist as the middle of their body have limited movements. The waist is not a weight bearing structure or a place from which to move; it is a term used in the clothing industry. The middle of our bodies is found at our hip joints.

When you are sitting at balance, you will feel light and peaceful. There will be minimal muscular work needed to hold you upright. Instead, your muscles will be free to move in any direction needed to create the sounds you desire.

Chapter 5
Spatial Relationship to the Piano
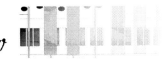

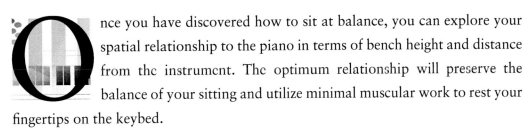nce you have discovered how to sit at balance, you can explore your spatial relationship to the piano in terms of bench height and distance from the instrument. The optimum relationship will preserve the balance of your sitting and utilize minimal muscular work to rest your fingertips on the keybed.

Your arm structure is attached to your torso at the sternoclavicular joint, where the collarbone meets the breastbone. The structure is suspended over the ribs by virtue of a vast system of connective tissue. This tissue covers the bones and muscles and acts like a tenting device to keep your arms in a neutral position. You don't have to hold your arms up when they are resting at your sides; the connective tissue provides this buoyancy and support. If you consider your forearm as a sort of lever, you can bend at the elbow and rest your weight through your fingertips into the keybed. The most efficient way to achieve this "resting lever" feeling is to sit at a height that allows your forearms to be parallel to the floor. Any position higher than this would incur a holding up of the upper arm and a dropping of the wrist. This could cause unnecessary tension in the upper back and possible strain to the wrist joint. A bench height lower than optimum could cause slouching of the torso and holding up in the wrist—equally undesirable. When sitting at the appropriate height, the weight and energy of your arm drops easily into the key with the aid of gravity. There is no unnecessary muscular tension to impede the movement of the arm down to play the key. There are also no breaks in the wrist joint which impede the unification of finger, hand, and arm.

When exploring bench distance from the piano, notice first where you are seated on the bench. Ideally, your placement will be on the front half of the bench. The weight of your legs will travel freely through the balance points of your knees and ankles into the floor. If you sit back too far, you will feel as if you are "sitting on your legs." It will be difficult to feel the floor with your feet and to use the contact with the floor for support and movement. Children and some shorter people need carpet squares or phone books under their feet, as their feet do not rest on the floor when seated on the front half of the bench. It is not advisable to sit further forward to reach the floor, as this will impair your center of gravity. You will feel like you are falling forward onto the piano. Simply place carpet squares or phone books on the floor to maintain a balanced position. Once you discover your seating placement on the bench, you can explore the bench distance from the piano. Ideally, your arms will be resting at your sides, elbows slightly in front of your torso, when your fingers are on the white keys. If your bench is too close, your arms will feel crowded by your torso. When your bench is placed too far back you will be reaching in front of your torso to get to the keys, thus utilizing upper arm muscles. The appropriate distance from the keyboard allows the muscles of the upper arm to be at rest when you are sitting with your fingers resting on the bottom of the keys. The muscles of the upper arm are then free to aid you in movement in any direction.

Many pianists describe a feeling of lightness when sitting balanced at the correct height and distance from the piano. They say it feels effortless or easy. Take the time you need in each practice and performing environment to find this perfect place.

Chapter 6
The Whole Arm

Many pianists are surprised to learn that their whole arm consists of a collarbone, a shoulder blade, an upper arm bone, two lower arm bones, a wrist, and a hand. It is also a revelation to learn that the skeletal system of the whole arm is attached to the body at the breastbone, not at the shoulder as many pianists think. With this information, you can begin to move from the joint where your arm attaches to your body, the sternoclavicular joint. This joint is named for the two bones that connect there: the collarbone (clavicle) and the breastbone (sternum).

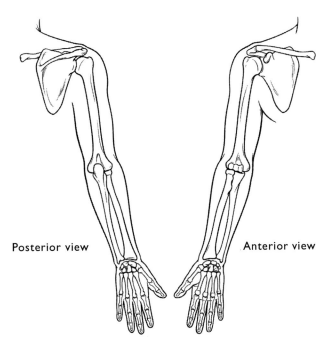

Posterior view   Anterior view

Figure 6.1. The Right Arm.

Although we are most aware of finger movement, there is actually a continuation of almost every movement at the piano to the sternoclavicular, or first arm, joint. Every fluid wrist movement, every arm movement away from the torso, every movement up or toward the fallboard requires a fluid follow-through to the first arm joint. To feel this joint, place the index finger of your right hand in the slight indentation just above your breastbone. Now feel the spongy area to the left of the indentation, against your collarbone. While touching this joint you can move your left arm across your chest and get a sense of the amount of movement available. Next, place your right palm over your left arm onto your left shoulder blade. Move your left arm across your body and notice that the shoulder blade moves with the collarbone. These two bones are connected and move together. We use this larger movement from the first arm joint when playing cross-hand passages.

To explore the full range of first arm joint movement, you must access your kinesthetic sense. The range includes movement up and down as well as forward and back. Close your eyes and move your whole arm structure up towards your ears—be careful not to scrunch your neck! Then allow your arms to drift back to a balanced position. A complex system of connective tissue keeps your arm structure suspended above your ribs. Thus, it should be possible to move the arm structure down from this balanced position a few inches. Many pianists carry their arm structure in a chronically low position and cannot move lower than where they feel their arms generally lie. This is due to a reconfiguration of the connective tissue caused by a mismapping of the arm structure as lower than it actually is. This mismapping leads to a habit of holding the shoulders down. Gentle range of motion exercises daily will help correct this. Remember that when the arm structure is suspended above the ribs, you can move up and down from neutral. To feel the range of back and forward movement, first bring your arms around front and give yourself a hug. Then gently move your shoulders back to a place where the shoulder joints are facing to the side. From there you can bring your shoulders back and feel your shoulder blades coming closer together. Then return to a place where your shoulder joints are facing to the side.

Of course the majority of movements from the sternoclavicular joint will not be very large when playing the piano. However, it is important to feel the micro-movement in this joint and in the surrounding structures. By being aware of this joint when playing, you reduce the incidence of "fixing" the arm at the shoulder. Any movement against a fixture creates strain and injury. By allowing arm movements to follow through to the place where the whole arm meets the torso, you avoid fixing. The anatomical term for this sequencing of arm joint movement is *humeroscapular rhythm*.[1] This term describes the movement of the arm from the humerus, or upper arm, through the clavicle (collarbone) and scapula (shoulder blade). Humeroscapular rhythm is used in piano playing when we travel laterally, for cross-hand passages, and in the vertical movements we use to play the keys. A helpful tool when exploring your awareness of micro-movement at the first arm joint is to ask a partner to place their hands on your shoulder blades as you play. Because the collarbone and shoulder blade are connected, any small movement at the sternoclavicular joint can be felt in the shoulder blade. You will feel the movement more with a partner's hands on your shoulder blades.

---

1. Most medical references refer to this sequencing as *scapulohumeral rhythm*, reflecting the common naming order of anatomical structures from the bone nearest to the body to the bone farther away from the body. Barbara Conable coined the term *humeroscapular rhythm* to explain the sequencing of movement from the upper arm and shoulder joint to the sternoclavicular joint where the whole arm attaches to the torso.

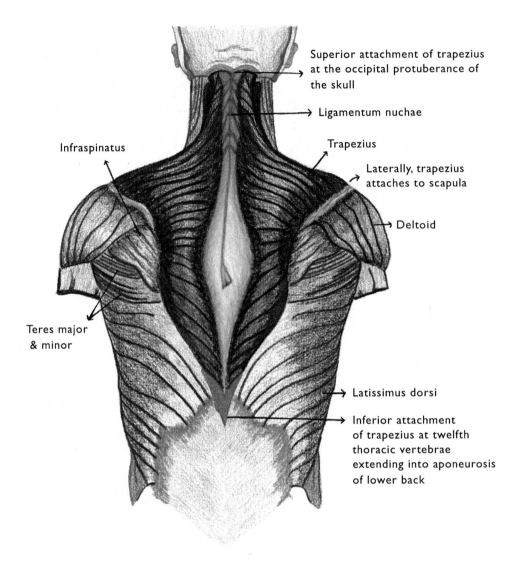

Superior attachment of trapezius
at the occipital protuberance of
the skull

Ligamentum nuchae

Trapezius

Laterally, trapezius
attaches to scapula

Deltoid

Infraspinatus

Teres major
& minor

Latissimus dorsi

Inferior attachment
of trapezius at twelfth
thoracic vertebrae
extending into aponeurosis
of lower back

Figure 6.2. The Back.

The trapezius muscle, that trapezoid-shaped muscle that begins in your neck and continues across your back, will become tight if there is not enough movement at the first arm joint. This is caused by holding the muscle still or trying to move just from the shoulder due to an incorrect body map of the whole arm. The Alexander

Technique teaches that tension in the neck affects the freedom of all muscles below it. Keep awareness of the quality of the neck muscles and the upper back muscles as you play.

There are several other important joints in the arm that we will explore in subsequent chapters addressing specific elements of piano technique. For now, do your best to find the balance of your arm structure and feel movement at the sternoclavicular joint throughout the day. You can notice this movement as you reach for an object, if you are swimming or dancing, and every time your arms reach above your head or across your body.

Chapter 7
Breathing

Since the correlation between breath and sound is not as direct for pianists as for singers and wind players, it may be overlooked, but good breathing is just as important for a pianist as for any other musician. Through our breathing, we provide sufficient oxygen to our bodies and keep our nervous systems in repose, our mental faculties clear, our muscles strong and flexible, and our vital organs functioning at peak capacity. Good breathing is also good for our music: it can help shape our musical phrasing.

Air enters our body without conscious direction, unless we intend to take in air to match the phrase we are singing or playing on a wind instrument. This automatic process of inhalation is governed by chemoreceptors in our brain, which sense an excess of carbon dioxide. When the levels of this gas become too high, a message is sent to the muscles of the ribs—the intercostal muscles—and to the thoracic diaphragm. Intercostal muscles swing the ribs up and out and the thoracic diaphragm descends, creating an expansion of the thoracic cavity. As the volume of the thoracic cavity increases, the pressure drops resulting in a vacuum that brings air into our lungs, providing oxygen. Thus, we do not need to draw, swallow, or suck air into our lungs. It is important to note that the lungs do not push the ribs open, rather the ribs and diaphragm move so the lungs can fill with air and expel air.

Although breathing will continue without conscious control, bringing awareness to breathing will increase the power of the breath to relax and focus you. Your brain is fully equipped to include breathing in the task of music making. The sensory feedback provided by the structures in your body that feel the air and move for respiration provide the key for increasing this awareness. Begin by using the sensory feedback provided by the structures in your body that actually feel the air you are breathing. Then, learn to feel clearly the movements involved in respiration.

We can feel air entering our bodies through our nose or mouth. The lining of our nostrils and mouth contains many tactile receptors that give us information about the temperature and humidity of the air we breathe. To feel this sensation more acutely, blow on the back of your hand. Our kinesthetic receptors in the intercostal muscles allow us to feel our ribs moving up and out, creating space for the lungs to fill with air when we inhale. Upon exhalation, we feel the ribs moving down and in. The "breathing joints," where the ribs meet the spine in back and cartilage connects ribs to the breastbone in front, are where this movement occurs. If you have difficulty feeling rib movement, tie a scarf around the upper part of your chest and feel the rib movement against it. Most people misunderstand, or mismap, the location of the lungs. It is important to realize that they reside in the upper part of the torso from just above the collarbones (clavicles) to the lower tip of the breastbone (sternum). The lungs are lower in the back than in the front. The apex, or top, of the lungs is above the collarbones, and this contributes to the buoyancy of the arm structure as you breathe. When the arm structure is balanced and free of downward pull, it will rise and fall subtly with inhalation and exhalation.

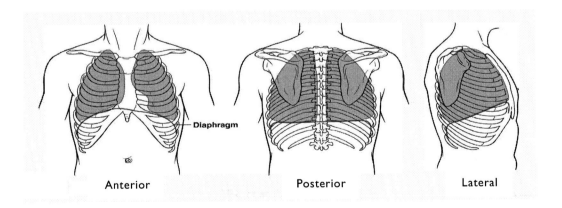

Figure 7.1. Views of the Lungs.

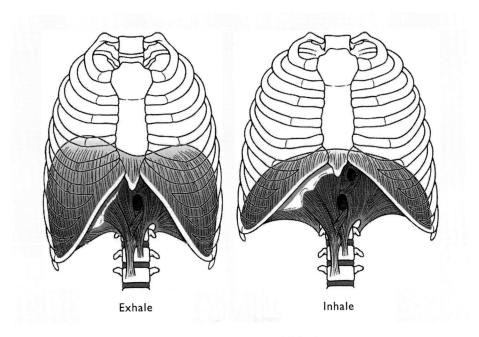

Exhale   Inhale

Figure 7.2. Frontal View of Diaphragm.

As the ribs move up and out, the thoracic diaphragm also responds to the chemoreceptors, descending and pushing out the contents of our abdominal cavity against the muscular wall that surrounds it. We can't really feel the diaphragm itself, as it has so few sensory receptors, but we can feel our abdominal wall expanding 360 degrees around. To enhance this sensation, place your hands on the front and back of your abdomen as you breathe in. Expansion of the abdominal wall as you inhale should not be hampered at any time by artificial "holding in" of the stomach. When we exhale, these abdominal muscles should be free of tension and rebound to their rest position. The kinesthetic sensation of the wave of breathing for inhalation and exhalation continues to the floor of the pelvis. The muscles here push down as contents of the pelvic cavity are displaced from the pressure above as we inhale. When we exhale, these muscles rebound as the contents of the pelvic cavity move back up. To feel the location of the pelvic floor more clearly, cough while sitting. The gentle pressure against your seat is from the muscles of the pelvic floor.

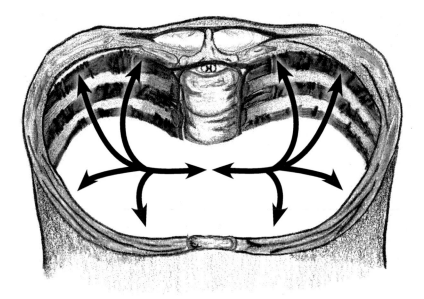

Figure 7.3. The abdominal wall expands 360 degrees around during inhalation.

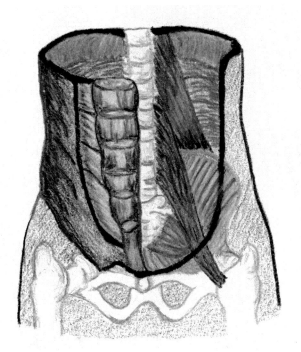

Figure 7.4. The muscles of the abdominal cavity extend from the base of the ribs to the top of the pelvis.

The spine participates in the movements of breathing for both inhalation and exhalation. As we inhale, the spine gathers and shortens by about one-eighth to one-fourth of an inch. This makes sense, as our bodies are slightly widening with the expansion of the chest and abdomen. If we are getting wider, our height must correspondingly decrease if our mass stays the same. When we exhale, our spines lengthen as our torsos become slightly narrower. To feel the spinal movement for breathing, sit in a chair and curl your torso down over your legs, dangling your arms at your side. As you breathe in, your head will rise up a bit as your spine shortens, or gathers. Conversely, when you exhale the spine lengthens and your head will move back down. You may be able to feel these movements better while draped over an exercise ball. Spinal gathering and lengthening with the breath combines with spinal movements that support the arms. Free spines also change in shape as a natural part of movement, and that alteration is experienced as support for the limbs. When a difficult passage arises, the pianist may choose to lengthen the spine to generate the necessary freedom to execute the passage.

Breathing, as described here, occurs in a wave that travels in the same direction when inhaling and exhaling. In a general sense, the movement starts at the top of our torsos and travels down for both aspects of the breathing cycle. Upon inhalation, our ribs move up and out, the thoracic diaphragm descends, the abdominal wall is pushed out all around, and the pelvic floor descends. When we exhale, the ribs move down and in, the thoracic diaphragm and abdominal wall spring back to rest position, and the pelvic floor springs back up. The spinal movements of gathering and lengthening occur alongside the wave of movements for inhalation and exhalation. The spinal gathering and lengthening is probably a result of an alteration of the spine's curves.

As you begin to feel the movements of breathing when you play and in everyday life, you will cultivate a habit of awareness that will support your music making. When your breathing is free and easy, the nervous system is relaxed and focused. The muscles in your body will be less fatigued as they will be adequately oxygenated. You will be able to create expansion in your phrases and feel the music moving with more fluidity. It is not necessary to match your breath to each phrase, although this is a choice. Some pianists choose to coordinate their breathing with singers or wind players they collaborate with. Breathing can also be used as a cue in ensemble playing. By simply keeping your breath free and easy, you will be able to feel the rhythm and phrase direction more clearly. Some pianists mark breathing cues in their music to remind themselves to breathe during rests, long notes, or before a difficult passage.

Organize your practice routine to include a few minutes of breathing awareness before you play. Sit quietly, at balance, and feel all of the movements described in this chapter for inhalation and exhalation. This practice is the best preparation for any performance as well.

Part II
Piano Technique

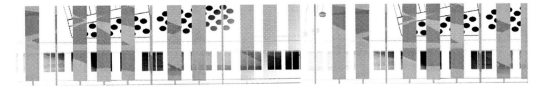

Chapter 8
The Neutral Hand

The neutral hand is free of unnecessary flexion, extension, abduction, or adduction of the fingers. To discover your neutral hand, allow your arm to hang by your side as you sit at the piano. Notice the natural curve of the fingers that gravity allows. It is not necessary to hold a hand position to achieve the natural curve created by the relationship of various joints in your hand. Keeping your arm hanging at your side, use your kinesthetic sense, accessing awareness of the quality and movement of your joints, tendons, and muscles. First, curl your hand as if holding a ball—this is flexion of the fingers. Next, straighten your fingers—this is extension of the fingers. Now stretch your hand open, fingers wide apart, creating abduction. And finally, press all the fingers tightly together in the movement called adduction. Notice how each of these activities requires effort or work and maybe even some discomfort. Now return to the neutral hand and experience through your kinesthetic sense the absence of any muscular activity. It is almost a feeling of "nothing" in the hand.

The neutral hand is the hand to bring to the piano when you begin to play. As you play, muscular activity will be required. You will need to use some flexion, extension, abduction, and adduction of the fingers. However, if you use a mid-range of movement for these activities and return to the neutral hand as much as possible, you will be less likely to strain or fatigue your hand. A mid-range of movement is just that—a movement within the fullest extent of the possible range. Thus, you would not want to overstretch your hand for chords. At times, your hand may need to be open for chords or arpeggios. This can be accomplished by opening from the carpometacarpal joint—where the finger bones meet the wrist joint—and from the metacarpophalangeal joint—the large knuckle of the fingers (see Figure 14.1 on page 86). Many pianists mistakenly try to open their hand only from the larger knuckle, ignoring the space available for opening between each long finger bone that lies in the hand. You can access this space between each of the fingers by opening your hand like a fan. A more passive, less "stretched" opening is accomplished by using your other hand to open the space between each finger. Return to your body map of the fingers to be sure you understand that they begin at the wrist joint, not the web space between the fingers. It may be desirable to curl the fingers within mid-range to achieve a specific sound or skill, such as a trill or repeated notes. As long as you return again and again to the neutral hand position and stay within the mid-range of joint movement, you will not create unnecessary tension.

Be aware of the nature and quality of the non-playing fingers. Often, a curled fifth finger or a stretched thumb compromises the neutral hand. Watch and feel the non-playing fingers as you practice. They should follow the direction of the fingers that play, not move in an opposite direction. Notice the release of the playing finger and encourage it to come along with the rest of the hand after playing a note.

When teaching, avoid the term "hand position," which might encourage holding the hand in a shape. Instead, describe and encourage kinesthetic exploration of the neutral hand. Explore within the literature places where flexing, curling, abduction, and adduction might be necessary. Remember to describe and demonstrate the mid-range movements. With young children, observe for the tendency to want to place each finger over the note of a passage or pentascale. This "position" is actually an abduction of the small hand and can lead to chronic tension.

Many pianists are taught to always keep their thumb on the keyboard. This can lead to fixing the thumb and compression of the wrist due to chronic twisting. When playing a white note passage, the thumb may rest next to the second finger, off of the keyboard. To determine where the thumb should rest, return to observing your hand hanging by your side. There is a relationship between the thumb and second finger that can be maintained often when playing, the exception being when the hand is open for chords and arpeggios. The rest position of the thumb is a place to return to as much as possible. When teaching children, be aware that the smaller hand may allow for a resting of the thumb on the keys for white note passages.

By maintaining the neutral hand, unnecessary tension is avoided. The fingers are free to move into action from a neutral place, and there is less danger of strain or injury.

Chapter 9
The Piano Map

Identification of the major visible parts of the piano responsible for sound production, and a basic understanding of how they work, will improve your ability to create musical effects. The parts of the modern grand piano we shall explore in this chapter include the metal plate, pin block and tuning pins, strings, soundboard, hammers, dampers, keys, and pedals (see Figure 9.1).

The metal plate is the heart of the piano's strength. It is large in surface area but very thin. This remarkable structure bears the stress of the strings and contributes more than one-third of the total weight of the modern grand piano. Nickel-plated tuning pins are used in the stringing process. The pin block is a very crucial part of the piano in that it holds the tuning pins tight. Twisting tuning pins clockwise increases tension and raises pitch, and turning them counterclockwise conversely lowers the pitch. The bridges located on top of the soundboard transmit the vibrations of the strings to the soundboard to greatly amplify the sound of the vibrating strings. These vibrations are then released into the air and captured by the auditory system. Modern grand pianos are strung to provide a rich full tone with plenty of volume by using combinations of strings to produce all but the lowest bass notes. There are three strings per note in the top five octaves or so, usually two strings per note in the high bass, and one string per note in the lowest bass notes. The strings are made of pure carbon steel and can withstand repeated strikes by the hammer without distortion. Frequency of vibration, or pitch, is inversely proportional to the length of the string. Thus, the lower strings vibrate more slowly and are longer. Thickness also affects the rate of vibration but in a direct proportion—the thicker the string, the slower the vibration and, consequently, the lower the pitch. By adding thickness to the bass strings with wound copper wire, variables of length and mass combine to accommodate pitch. The copper wire is rust-resistant and produces a good tone for the lower register.

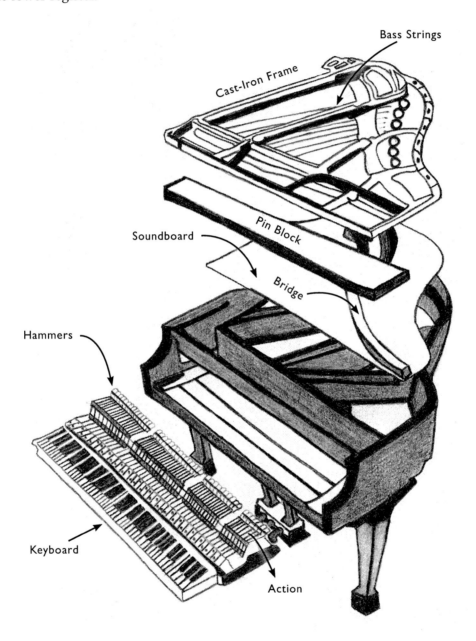

Figure 9.1. Parts of the Modern Grand Piano.

On a horizontal plane to the floor beneath the plate is the soundboard. The soundboard is a thin, flexible diaphragm made of spruce wood, glued at its edges to a wooden frame. It has ribs underneath maintaining the curvature and bridges attached to the upper surface. By attaching strings to the bridges, their vibrations are transmitted to the largest area of the soundboard, increasing volume dramatically. Spruce is the preferred wood used in soundboard production because of its superior vibrating qualities.

Hammers are one of the distinguishing elements between the modern piano and its precursors. The invention of the modern piano is credited to Bartolomeo Cristofori of Padua, Italy. The three Cristofori pianos still in existence date from the 1720s. Before hammers, tangents (small metal blades) in a clavichord would strike the strings, or quills in a harpsichord would pluck the strings. Cristofori's great success was in solving the fundamental problem of piano design: how the hammers strike and rebound from the strings. The hammer must strike the string but not remain in contact with it, as this would dampen the sound. The hammer must also return to its rest position without bouncing violently, and it must be possible to repeat a note rapidly. Cristofori's solutions to these problems led the way to sound production on the modern grand piano. When we depress the key, a complex series of events are set into motion, resulting in the hammers striking the strings.

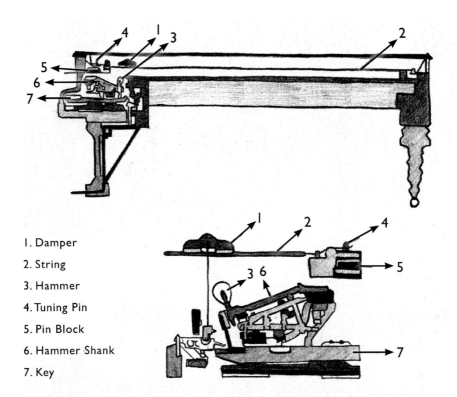

1. Damper
2. String
3. Hammer
4. Tuning Pin
5. Pin Block
6. Hammer Shank
7. Key

Fingers press key on keyboard, which is connected to the hammer through the central rail and hammer shank. The hammer strikes the string depending on how much the finger depresses the key.

Figure 9.2. Parts of the Piano Keys.

Sitting on the top of the strings are the dampers, keeping the strings from vibrating. When the hammer is about halfway to the string, the damper begins to lift, allowing the string to vibrate. The dampers lift individually with each hammer and as a group with the sustain pedal. When a key or the sustain pedal is released, the dampers return to the string, stopping the vibration.

The keys on a grand piano extend far beyond the portion visible in front of the fallboard—up to a couple of feet long in a concert grand piano. One reason grand and upright pianos feel so different is the length of the key. Upright piano keys can be half that length, and spinets even shorter. The distance the key travels is a fundamental part of touch, usually in the neighborhood of three-eighths to one-half of an inch. Many pianists mistakenly aim their weight and energy to a much deeper place, sometimes underneath the base of the keyboard. This can result in a hard landing on the bottom of the key with such force that the finger and arm receive a "kickback," or opposing movement that can cause injury.

Another factor with potential for injury to the pianist is when the key weight or touch weight is too heavy. To avoid injury, try to practice on an instrument with a proper touch weight, reasonably uniform in each register. With touch weight problems, it is important to have a technician diagnose and determine possible solutions. An average touch weight is about fifty to sixty grams, though quite often the bass will be heavier and the treble lighter. It is possible to roughly check the touch weight of the pianos you play most often with a stack of nickels. Each nickel weighs approximately five grams, so you will need a stack of about twelve to test your piano. To measure the touch weight on your piano, first depress the damper pedal to lift the dampers. Then place a stack of ten nickels gently on the edge of the white key. The key should travel down to the point of sound, that place about three-quarters of the way down the key depth where you feel a slight bump if you depress the key silently. This is where the hammer is released to strike the string. If needed, you can add more nickels to the stack until the key travels down to this point. Check the touch weight on many keys in many different registers for uniformity. Many factors affect touch weight or the perception of touch weight: poor geometry, improper friction, and material problems in the action or maladjustment of action parts. If the piano does not feel right, it is well worth having it evaluated by a qualified technician.

The pedals of the grand piano have different effects and applications. The far left pedal, or *una corda*, reduces volume or changes the sound by shifting the keyboard and action slightly to the right so that the hammers strike one less string. Thus, where there are three strings, two are struck by the hammer; where there are two strings, one is struck; and in the low bass the hammer strikes the single string on the left side. Tone color is also affected by the *una corda* since a softer area of the hammer is striking the string, producing a more ethereal or muted sound. The term *una corda* is confusing, as it originated with earlier pianos in the late eighteenth and nineteenth centuries, which were strung with two strings per note rather than three. Thus, shifting the action caused the hammers to strike one string—hence the term *una corda*. On the modern grand piano, the strings are too close together to achieve this effect, and usually two of the three strings are left to vibrate in the middle register. The common term used by composers for release of the *una corda* is *tre corde*, or three strings. On some instruments, the *una corda* pedal can be depressed halfway for another variation in sound.

The middle pedal, or sostenuto pedal, sustains only the notes that are held down before it is depressed. Once the middle pedal is depressed, dampers of held keys remain lifted and these notes will sustain until the pedal is released. This is a helpful tool for sustaining long bass notes below a series of chords requiring both hands. It is possible to use the sostenuto pedal and the damper pedal at the same time by operating the sostenuto pedal with the left foot.

The far right pedal is the sustain pedal. When depressed, it lifts all of the dampers from the strings simultaneously, allowing them to vibrate freely. This serves two purposes. First, it assists the pianist in producing a musical legato, connecting sounds difficult or impossible to connect physically; and secondly, it greatly increases the volume of the piano and enriches the tonal combinations. It is possible to access several levels of the sustain pedal for varying effects. Often, a half pedal is required to sustain the sound without blurring the melodic line. This technique can be used to interpret Chopin's pedal markings, as his piano was much less resonant than the modern grand. A quarter pedal can be used for even less collection of sound. There are several ways to time the depression and release of the damper pedal. Very often it is depressed in a syncopated fashion—after the note or chord is sounded. The syncopated pedal connects units of sound without blurring. A flutter pedal, or partial releases of the pedal, can dissolve sound slowly beneath a melody or chord that is sustained. It is also possible to create a slow decay of sound by a slow release of the damper pedal.

Movement of the foot in pedaling occurs at the ankle joint. The ankle joint is not the two bumps felt on either side of the lower leg above the foot. Those two bumps are the ends of the lower leg bones—the tibia and fibula. To locate the ankle joint, palpate the space in front where the lower leg bones meet the foot bones. The heel acts as a fulcrum for movement of the foot against the pedal. This movement sequences up the leg and has a follow through to the knee and hip joints. If we move just the foot, we will develop soreness in the shins and tension in the knees and hips. Similarly, if we initiate pedaling movement from the knee or hip, we will cause tension and create fatigue in our legs.

As pianists and teachers, we will benefit greatly from increasing our knowledge of the construction and sound production system of our instruments. Many a pianist has been injured from a misunderstanding of where and how tone, dynamics, and articulation occur. Just as knowledge of our bodies improves our movement, so does knowledge of our instruments improve our use of the piano.

Chapter 10
Tone Production

Otto Ortmann and Tobias Matthay studied the process of tone production at the piano in great detail in the early twentieth century. Dorothy Taubman and her followers picked up the thread from these pioneers and developed a system of piano technique named the Taubman Approach. Many of the ideas presented in this chapter stem from my eight years of study with the Taubman faculty. I am very grateful for all I have learned from them and for what they have contributed to the world of piano technique.

In his book *The Physical Basis of Piano Touch and Tone*, published in 1925, Otto Ortmann wrote: "Differences in touch, so far as they affect vibration of the string, always involve differences of key descent."[2] By applying physical properties to the production of tone at the piano, he discovered that the fundamental properties of a moving body are mass, direction, and speed. His conclusion was that "for any given key the mass is fixed, the direction for all keys is fixed: the only remaining variable is speed."[3] Thus, to create a louder sound, a greater speed into the key is required; and a slower key descent will result in the hammer striking the string more gently, yielding a softer sound.

A newer way of thinking about this combination of variables has emerged in the piano pedagogy literature of the twenty-first century. I am indebted to my colleague Douglas Johnson of the Berklee College of Music for opening my eyes to the possibility of applying a physics equation directly to the discussion of dynamics created at the piano. His theory is that dynamics are a result of the physical property of force, which

---

2. Otto Ortmann, *The Physical Basis of Piano Touch and Tone* (New York: E. P. Dutton & Co., 1925), 33.
3. Ibid., 15.

is defined as mass times acceleration. This equation takes into account the speed of movement into the key as well as the total body mass involved with the movement. I have since discovered that when playing very softly it is easier to slowly depress a key if my body is still. This stillness results in less mass and energy of my body being involved with the key descent. Movements from my fingers still sequence up through my arm, as my body is not stiff—just quiet. Conversely, for the loudest sounds I make at the piano, I must use the weight of my entire arm and also call upon my spine for support so that more energy can be delivered into the key. Another source of mass and energy for loud sounds is a solid connection with feeling our feet on the floor. This connection affords the possibility of mobilizing weight and energy from the ground up. A bright awareness of free breathing enhances ease in playing loud sounds. When our breathing is free, our muscles are more relaxed and we can call upon more of the mass of our arms to be delivered into the key. A helpful corollary to creating loud sounds is a statement made by my Taubman teacher, Robert Durso. He said: "Forte equals freedom." In truth, it takes more control to descend slowly into the key for a pianissimo effect than to drop freely with gravity for a forte effect.

It is important to note that the quality of the sound is also affected by the speed of the key descent. Even when creating a loud sound, it is most often desirable to achieve a beautiful tone. Thus, it is often taught in the Taubman Approach to release more arm weight and aim to the point of sound to produce a loud sound. This instruction eliminates the possibility of a harsh tone and the callused or bleeding fingertips that result from a very rapid key descent. Because the energy is released before the finger reaches the bottom of the key, there is actually a slight slowing in key descent after the point of sound, which is barely perceptible and happens automatically when aiming to the point of sound rather than the keybed. The point of sound can be felt as a slight bump one-eighth to one-fourth of an inch from the bottom of the key. According to Tobias Matthay in his book *The Act of Touch in All Its Diversity* (1903), a harsh sound quality results as follows: "It is found that a too sudden application of energy tends to cause the string to move off rather into segmental vibration, than into those complete vibrations—of its whole length—

60

that enforce the fundamental sound."[4] What this means is that fewer overtones are released if the key is depressed too rapidly, and the sound is hollow and dies away quickly. It is important to learn to listen to the sound after you play to determine if it is round and full of overtones or sharp and decaying quickly.

Another important aspect of tone production is the realization that all sound creation from a given key is completed at the moment the string is set into vibration by the hammer. Thus, any finger movement on the bottom of the key, short of rebound to the next key, is useless. Unnecessary movements on the keybed, such as pressing or vibrating, can cause fatigue and injury. These unnecessary movements also make it difficult to rebound to the next key. The quality of the finger, hand, and arm in contact with the keybed should be akin to balanced resting.

Other variations in sound production are created by articulation. In short, the key descent affects dynamics and the key release affects articulation. For a legato effect the key is released slowly in time with the descent of the next key. There is a feeling of "walking along the bottom" of the key as your arm weight is transferred continuously from key bottom to key bottom. It is a revelation to many pianists to experience legato as a product of timing rather than "holding" or "squeezing." Staccato is achieved by releasing the key promptly, thus allowing the key to rebound as soon as tone production occurs. Staccato can be felt as a slight bouncing off the bottom of the key. The space between staccato notes can be varied to create a portato effect.

Clearly, as stated by Ortmann, vertical action on the keys is the only action capable of producing sound. The horizontal movements of the arms are used to take us across the keys. Vertical and horizontal movements often occur at different speeds, allowing us to play soft passages quickly and loud passages slowly. An important addition to this point is that the finger must be directly over the key before it is depressed. This is especially important for the successful playing of leaps. We use our kinesthetic sense combined with rotational movements and the lateral arm

---

4. Tobias Matthay, *The Act of Touch in All Its Diversity* (London: Bosworth & Co. Ltd., 1903), 74–75.

movements to learn the distance of a leap "by feel." Sometimes pianists feel they do not have time to get to the note before they play it. Keep in mind that if you are over the note before you play it, you will never miss it!

Tone production is the essential palette that pianists work from to create their own unique sound. It is important that we understand how to create variance in tone, articulation, and dynamics from a solid foundation of mechanics and movement.

Chapter 11
Rotation

When the term *rotation* is used in piano technique, it implies a combination of movements involving several different arm joints. These movements include forearm rotation and an outward movement of the whole arm. Rotation in piano technique is used for playing the thumb and fifth finger, and also for change of direction, trills, tremolos, leaps, and scale crossings. An essential movement for pianists, it was first described in *The Act of Touch in All Its Diversity* by Tobias Matthay in 1903: "Invisible adjustments of the Forearm are constantly required in a *rotary or tilting* direction, to ensure the Evenness of effect from all the fingers; and also to enable the fingers at either side of the hand to pronounce their notes prominently."[5] Dorothy Taubman explored this concept in depth while developing the Taubman Approach, beginning in 1940. There are several benefits to using rotation in piano technique. It is a rapid and efficient movement and also unifies the fingers, wrist, and arm. It can be combined with horizontal arm movements to accommodate distance and with vertical movements to control key depression and release.

To understand piano technique rotation, it is first necessary to explore the anatomy of the arm. Beginning with forearm rotation, note that the ulna is the axis around which the radius moves. The relationship between the two bones of the right forearm is shown in Figure 11.1. Notice that when the palm is facing up (right forearm supination), the two bones of the forearm are parallel to each other. When the palm is facing down (right forearm pronation), the radius and ulna are crossed.

---

5. Matthay, *The Act of Touch*, 202–203.

The muscles used for rotation—the pronators and supinators—are attached to the bones of the forearm. We cannot see or palpate these muscles. Pianists often try to use superficial muscles to rotate the forearm, resulting in tension that interferes with freedom of movement. The muscles on the top and bottom of the forearm that can be easily palpated are primarily for opening, closing, curling, and straightening the fingers, and for moving the wrist.

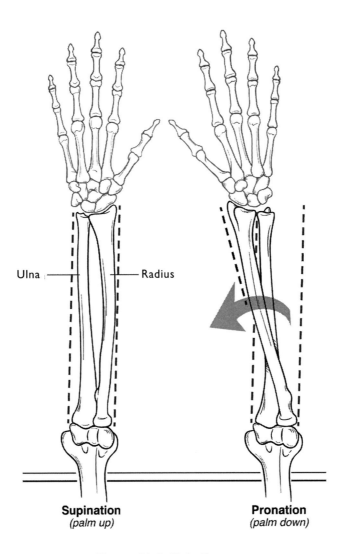

Figure 11.1. Right Forearm.

Forearm rotation can be used for playing the thumb. To ensure that this movement is free of tension, it is important to know where the thumb contacts the key so that the wrist will not be too low. The wrist should feel long and free, not shortened or compressed. Key contact for the thumb should be on the side of the thumb, near the middle of the nail. When playing black keys the contact point is slightly lower than that, near the base of the nail. In order to access forearm rotation when playing the thumb, it is necessary to have a preparatory movement before playing the key (Figure 11.2). I like to compare this concept to pulling back the bow before shooting an arrow. This preparatory movement involves moving the thumb, hand, and forearm away from the key you wish to play. Thus, for the left hand, as shown in Figure 11.2, the preparatory movement would be a slight tilt of the thumb, hand, and forearm from the elbow to the left, about forty-five degrees. The preparatory movement is an active movement, which is followed by a more passive movement: using gravity and falling back to the right to play the key (Figure 11.3).

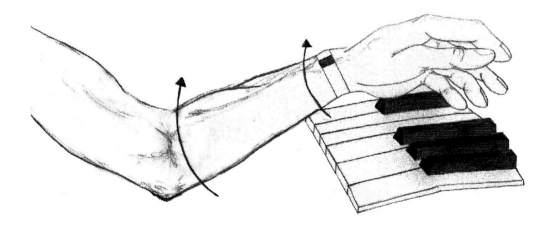

Figure 11.2. Preparation to 1 using forearm rotation (left hand).

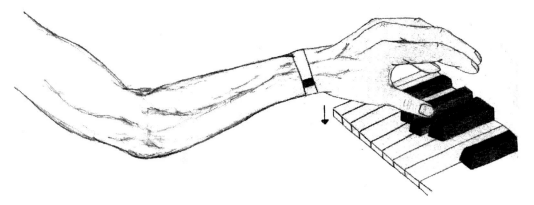

Figure 11.3. Thumb plays with forearm rotation (left hand).

Abduction (moving away from the body) of the arm is used when playing the fifth finger with piano technique rotation. Because rotation in piano technique involves a combination of movements from several joints in the arm, it has a different meaning than rotation when used to describe the anatomical turning movement of the forearm. Playing the fifth finger also requires a preparatory movement that involves the whole arm. To prepare to play the fifth finger, the arm is first pulled slightly away from the body. Thus, the preparatory movement for the fifth finger involves moving the elbow out slightly to the side and bringing the arm, wrist, hand, and finger as a unit away from the body. (Figure 11.4 provides a visualization of this movement for the right hand's fifth finger.) Then the whole arm swings back to play the key, aided by gravity (Figure 11.5). It is very important to allow the elbow and upper arm to return to a neutral place after playing the fifth finger. Sometimes the upper arm and elbow are left "holding out" to the side after playing the fifth finger, and this is undesirable, as it creates tension in the upper arm.

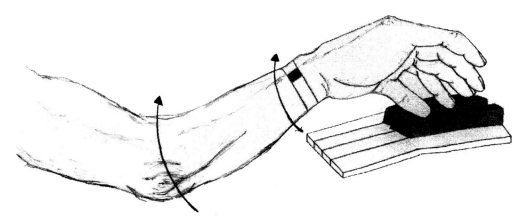

Figure 11.4. Preparation to 5 using a whole arm movement (right hand).

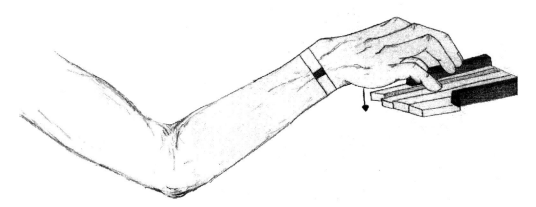

Figure 11.5. Playing 5 with whole arm movement (right hand).

A combination of forearm rotation and whole arm movements are used when rotating between two notes that change direction, and for trills and tremolos. To understand this concept, place your forearms on a table palms up. Rotating from the elbow, allow your palms to come down and rest on the table. This is the full range of forearm rotation. This movement is adequate for playing just the thumb, but not enough for moving from the thumb to another finger. When moving from the thumb to another finger, or back and forth between two adjacent fingers, we can combine the movements we have explored for the thumb and fifth finger. Use a preparatory movement and forearm rotation to play your thumb on the first note, then follow through with moving the elbow out to prepare to play the second note with your fifth finger. These movements tilt the finger, hand, and arm from side to side and result in the fingertips contacting the keys with a slight tilt. Rotation can be exaggerated when first learned in order to kinesthetically experience the movement. However, the movement will in time become quite small, almost invisible as Matthay described, unless you are using it for a leap.

Rotation is extremely useful for leaps, as it provides an efficient and unifying movement. This is particularly true when leaping towards the thumb, accessing forearm rotation. The rotational movement is combined with a lateral arm movement that takes you across the keys. A preparatory movement away from the note you are moving to is necessary to maintain the balance of the movement in both directions.

When playing scales or arpeggios, rotation can be used for crossings that occur in the direction toward the middle of the piano: ascending for the left hand and descending for the right hand. As you approach the scale crossing, remember the preparatory movement of the thumb. This turns the thumb, hand, and arm away from the next note. Forearm rotation then turns the hand and arm back to play the key. When playing the thumb, you will actually feel like you are "rolling over" the thumbnail. The finger that plays after the thumb will then turn back in the opposite direction, bringing the thumb out from underneath the hand.

To keep the rotational movements as free as possible, avoid ulnar deviation (twisting of the wrist) and stretching of the fingers. These activities tighten the superficial muscles of the forearm, inhibiting rotation. Also, keep in mind that the wrist does not rotate; it turns over as forearm rotation occurs at the elbow. Finger placement on the key affects the height of the wrist. In particular, if the thumb plays too low the wrist will drop, making rotation difficult and also straining the wrist joints.

The following examples explore rotation for change of direction, tremolos, and leaps.

Example 11.1. Mozart: Sonata in A Minor, K. 310, 1st movt.   Rotation: Change of Direction

Example 11.2. Mozart: Sonata in G Major, K. 283, 1st movt.   Rotation: Change of Direction

Example 11.3. Chopin: Etude in A Minor, Op. 25, No. 11   Rotation: Change of Direction

Example 11.4. Beethoven: Sonata in C Minor, Op. 13 ("Pathétique"), 1st movt.   Tremolo

Example 11.5. Chopin: Ballade No. 4 in F Minor, Op. 52   Legato Leaps

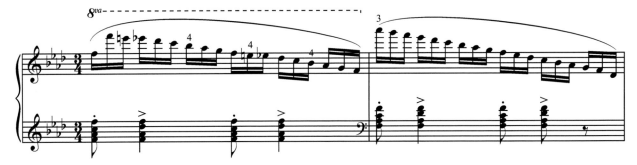

Example 11.6. Rachmaninoff: Prelude in B-flat Minor, Op. 32, No. 2   Legato Leaps

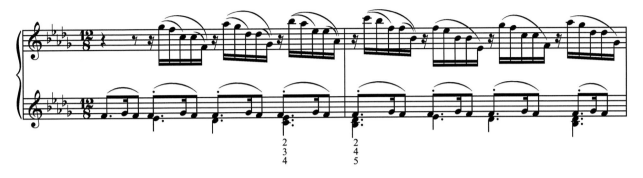

Example 11.7. Chopin: Nocturne in B-flat Minor, Op. 9, No. 1   Legato Leaps

Chapter 12
In and Out Movements

In and out movements include movements from the first arm joint and are used to move the whole arm in toward the black keys and out toward the body. This movement accommodates for the different lengths of our fingers and the varying lengths of the white and black keys. The in and out choreography prevents unnecessary curling or flexing of the fingers. By utilizing whole arm in and out movements, the wrist is also free of harmful twisting movements that are sometimes used to bring the thumb and second fingers toward the black keys. Pianists who do not use whole arm in and out movements often stretch or curl their fingers to get to the next note. This creates unnecessary tension in the hand. The neutral hand can be maintained by using whole arm movements to travel around the keyboard. In and out movements allow the arm to be present over each note or chord, supporting the fingers. Symbols used to designate this choreography in the examples that follow consist of arrows pointing up or down over the note that requires an in or out movement. The arrow pointing up refers to a movement in toward the fallboard and the arrow pointing down to a movement out toward the body.

When playing on all white keys, in and out is especially helpful to maintain the neutral hand. In movements are used to bring the shorter fingers toward the middle of the wide part of the white key and out movements for bringing the long fingers out to this same location. This is the spot where white key depression is best controlled. Example 12.1 shows a C major scale. When the right hand ascends, you move out to fingers 2 and 3, in for the thumb, out to fingers 2 and 3, and finally in to fingers 4 and 5. For the left hand ascending scale you move out to fingers 4 and 3, in to fingers 2 and 1, out to finger 3, and finally in to fingers 2 and 1. The descending scales have slightly different combinations of in and out movements, as shown in this example. These movements are very small and are connected by a smooth, lateral arm movement. Examples 12.2 and 12.3 are other instances of in and out movements for white key passages.

Example 12.1. C Major Scale In and Out on White Keys

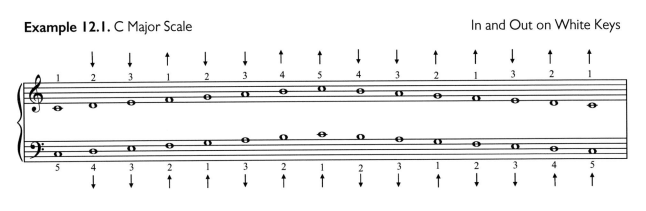

Example 12.2. Bach: Invention in C Major, BWV 772 In and Out on White Keys

Example 12.3. Mozart: Sonata in F Major, K. 533, 1st movt. In and Out on White Keys

In and out movements can also be used in passages with white and black keys to facilitate gradual movements toward the black keys. In Example 12.4, Bach's Invention in D Minor, BWV 775, the right hand and arm move in to prepare for the

fifth finger playing a black note in the first and fifth measure. Similarly, in Example 12.5, Mozart's Sonata in A Minor, K. 310, the fourth measure of the example shows an entire arpeggio that moves in to prepare for the following arpeggio, which has the thumb and fifth finger on black keys.

Example 12.4. Bach: Invention in D Minor, BWV 775   In and Out

Example 12.5. Mozart: Sonata in A Minor, K. 310, 1st movt.   In and Out

Example 12.6, Debussy's Arabesque No. 2, shows how a varied pattern contains a change of in and out movements to prepare for the combinations of black and white notes in the figure.

Sometimes the same note played by the same finger will require varying in and out approaches depending on the surrounding notes. The Mozart Piano Concerto in C Minor, K. 491, in Example 12.7 demonstrates this scenario. The fingering and the combinations of white and black notes determine the precise choreography of in and out movements.

Example 12.6. Debussy: Arabesque No. 2   In and Out

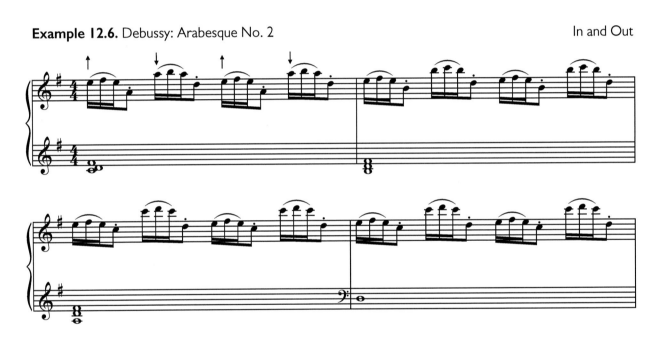

Example 12.7. Mozart: Piano Concerto in C Minor, K. 491, 3rd movt.   In and Out

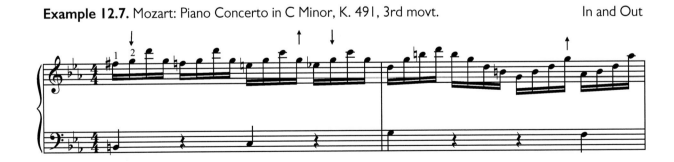

In and out is often necessary for passages with chords and intervals. It is essential that the whole arm move to be over the interval or chord before playing down. Intervals and chords require more weight than single notes. Example 12.8, Chopin's Ballade No. 2 in F Major, Op. 38, requires a complicated series of in and out movements in the right hand to ensure the weight of the arm is available for each interval.

Example 12.8. Chopin: Ballade No. 2 in F Major, Op. 38   Double Notes In and Out

Chapter 13
Spinal Support for the Arms

The spine supports lateral adjustments of the arm and torso by moving from side to side and from front to back. In fact, there are subtle spinal adjustments available for every note you play. These adjustments occur when we play in different registers of the piano. Remember that the head leads all spinal movement from the atlanto-occipital (AO) joint. The spine follows with movement evenly distributed across all of the vertebrae. Even a small spinal movement can be felt following through to the sacrum if the torso is free of unnecessary muscular tension.

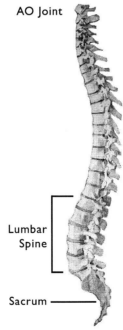

Figure 13.1. Parts of the Spine.

Using your kinesthetic sense, you can find the place for your spine that offers maximum support for the arms. In the bass region, the spine moves to the left, in the treble to the right. Through awareness of the contact of your feet with the floor, you can assist lateral spinal movements with your feet and legs. Pushing off from the floor with your right foot will move your torso to the left, and pushing off with the left foot will move your torso to the right. This organized whole body movement is more powerful and fluid than just moving your body laterally from the bench. When both hands are playing in opposite registers, the spine comes forward, and when both hands are in front of the body, the spine moves back. Examples 13.1–13.6 provide opportunities to explore movement of the spine as you move across the keyboard. Example 13.7 explores how the spine moves forward when the hands move out to treble and bass registers and then back when the hands play in front of the body.

There are a variety of positions available for the arm in relation to the spine across the range of the keyboard. Try to find the best alignment of your hand and arm for each passage. The position of best unification and mechanical advantage is found when the tip of the ulna (the boney knob behind the elbow) is behind the third finger. Imagine a line of support connecting these two places. To explore this alignment in any passage, allow your hand to rest in your lap; then bring your hand to the keyboard, allowing the arm to follow. This exercise keeps the upper arm from leading or holding out. The spine will adjust as you move to bring support to the arms.

In order for the finger, wrist, and arm to drop freely to the keybed, the elbow and forearm must be free of tension. Many pianists hold tension in these areas by mistakenly trying to hold their arms up and hold their hands on the keys. In fact, our spines assist in supporting the weight of our arms from above, and the keybed assists in supporting our arm weight from below. To examine your own kinesthetic awareness of these properties, notice how your elbows and forearms feel when you hold your arms above the keys. Next drop your arms by your sides and notice how they feel hanging freely. Finally, play a few notes or chords in each hand and rest on the bottom of the keys. This resting place should feel more like letting your arms hang at your sides, not like you are holding them up.

Example 13.1. Chopin: Etude in C Major, Op. 10, No. 1

Example 13.2. Ravel: *Jeux d'eau*

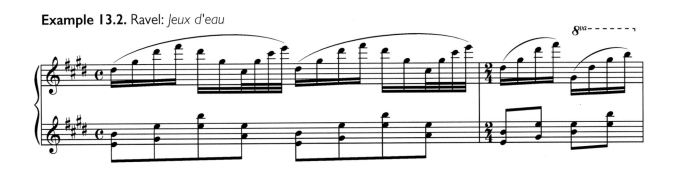

Example 13.3. Mozart: Piano Concerto in A Major, K. 488, 3rd movt.

Example 13.4. Debussy: "Clair de lune" from *Suite bergamasque*

Example 13.5. Chopin: Ballade No. 1 in G Minor, Op. 23

Example 13.6. Grieg: Piano Concerto in A Minor, Op. 16, 1st movt.

Example 13.7. Chopin: Ballade No. 2 in F Major, Op. 38

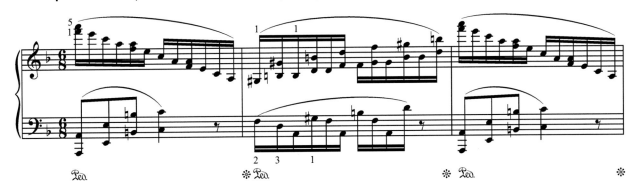

Chapter 14
Shaping

Shaping refers to the sequential adjustments of the joints of the fingers, wrist, and arm that allow for balance on each key, as well as to the smooth arm movements that take you to each key. The term was coined by Dorothy Taubman and was used at the Taubman Institute when choreographing passages. These adjustments are necessary due to the difference in the lengths of the fingers and the variation in height of the white and black keys. Shaping, as described above, is a physical activity and differs from musical shaping, which refers to the shape or direction of the line. Physical shaping supports and enhances musical shaping by adding inflection, direction, and tone color.

Each combination of fingers and black and white notes requires a slightly different balance point, which is reflected in the relationship of the joints of the fingers, wrist, and arm. It is particularly helpful to be aware of the movement across all of the wrist joints when exploring the variety of movements in physical shaping. Figure 14.1 shows the wrist joints as numbers 5 and 6. There is movement at these joints and also between the wrist bones, which allows for sequencing of wrist joint movements. To explore this concept, move your hands and wrists like a hula dancer. Another way to feel the sequencing of the wrist joints is to run your hands, palms down, back and forth over your kneecaps.

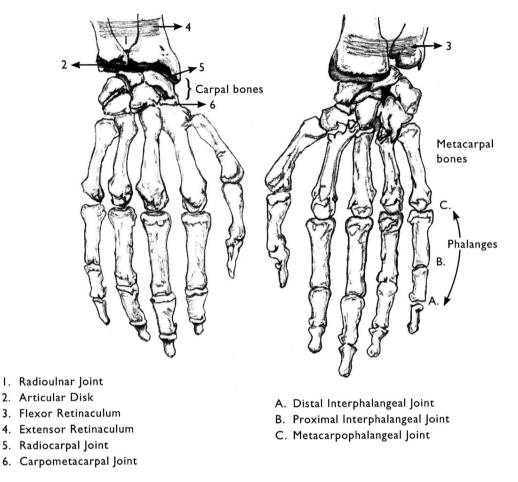

1. Radioulnar Joint
2. Articular Disk
3. Flexor Retinaculum
4. Extensor Retinaculum
5. Radiocarpal Joint
6. Carpometacarpal Joint

A. Distal Interphalangeal Joint
B. Proximal Interphalangeal Joint
C. Metacarpophalangeal Joint

Figure 14.1. Parts of the Hand.

Shaping is directly related to the natural curve of the hand and wrist, the relationship of the lengths of the fingers, and the combination of black and white notes. Terms used to describe shaping are under, over, forward, and back. These movements exist in a balanced, alternating relationship to each other. Under and over shapes are applied to passages that move across the keyboard. Over shapes are slightly higher than the flatter under shapes. These shapes would be employed when playing a D major scale. The wrist and arm will move up for an over shape when the long fingers 3 or 4 play the black notes. The wrist and arm will be slightly lower, using an under shape, for the white notes that are lower in space. When trying the examples, be sure that the over shapes (shown by a line curving over) are not too high and pulling you up off the keys. Similarly, the under shapes (shown by a line curving under) should not allow the wrist to dip below the arm.

Forward and back shapes apply to passages located in one hand position that do not move laterally. Forward shapes are higher and the fingertips contact the keys. Back shapes are lower and the pads of the fingers contact the keys. Explore this movement by placing your hands on a tabletop and moving your wrist and arm up to contact the fingertips and then down to access the pads of the fingers. Keep the contact point the same with the table throughout the exercise. The hand and arm do not move in and out when using forward and back shaping. In and out movements refer to arm movements taking you to different places on the keys (Chapter 12). Forward and back movements refer to different heights of the arm and wrist created by different finger/key contact points. In the examples, forward shapes are designated by a circled "F," and back shapes by a circled "B."

Shaping forward is used for repeated notes and chords to create a variation in color and a forward direction in the phrase. Often this forward shape is organized rhythmically around larger beats, with the arm beginning slightly lower than usual and moving forward slightly with each repetition until the rhythmic group is complete. Then the arm and hand return to the initial place to begin again. In Example 14.9, the repeated left hand chord pattern moves forward slightly through each dotted quarter note and then returns to a flat position for the next large beat. In Example 14.10, the forward shapes of repeated octaves and chords in the left hand organize best with the rhythm of the melody. Thus, in measure 1 the forward shape in the left hand organizes around a half note, then a quarter note. For measures 2, 5, and 6 the left hand forward shape organizes around a dotted quarter note to match the right hand melody.

Example 14.1. Mozart: Piano Concerto in C Major, K. 467, 3rd movt.   Under and Over

Example 14.2. Mozart: Piano Concerto in C Major, K. 467, 1st movt.   Under and Over

Example 14.3. Mozart: Piano Concerto in C Minor, K. 491, 1st movt.   Under and Over

Example 14.4. Chopin: Ballade No. 1 in G Minor, Op. 23   Under and Over

Example 14.5. Beethoven: Sonata in C-sharp Minor, Op. 27, No. 2   Under and Over
("Moonlight"), 3rd movt.

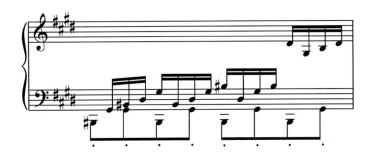

Example 14.6. Beethoven: Piano Concerto No. 3 in C Minor, Op. 37, 1st movt.   Under and Over

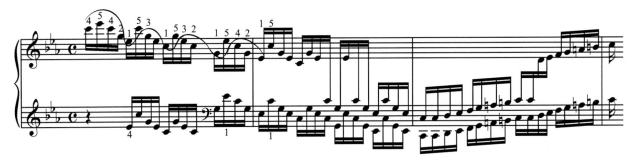

Example 14.7. Haydn: Sonata in E-flat Major, Hob. XVI:52, 1st movt.   Back and Forward

Example 14.8. Haydn: Sonata in E-flat Major, Hob. XVI:52, 1st movt.   Back and Forward

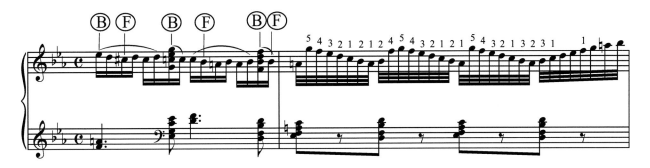

Example 14.9. Beethoven: Sonata in G Major, Op. 31, No. 1, 2nd movt.   Repeated Notes

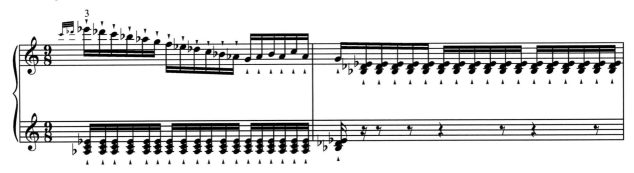

Example 14.10. Beethoven: Sonata in E-flat Major, Op. 27, No. 1, 2nd movt.   Repeated Notes

Chapter 15
Octaves and Chords

To effectively play octaves and chords, the body must be free of unnecessary tension in the back, abdomen, and arm muscles. Tension in any of these areas affects the free fall with gravity required to release the weight and energy of the arm into the piano. The more notes played simultaneously, the more energy needed to depress the keys. As we cannot change the weight of our arms, we rely upon the speed of our arm's descent to gather more energy. The freer the fall of the arm, the faster the fall and the more energy accumulated. For chords and octaves we need to access maximum freedom of the arm drop. If muscular force is employed, the contact with the keybed may be very hard and can result in injury to the fingertips as well as a harsh tone.

Begin exploring octaves and chords by sitting at balance, being certain that your skeletal system is supporting and bearing your weight and that your muscles are free for movement. It is especially helpful to gain kinesthetic awareness of the anterior portion of your spine, the core of your body, as you sit. This is the portion of your spine that supports the weight of your head and torso and delivers it into the bench through the pelvis and rockers. The lengthening and gathering of your spine also gives you support and freedom. One of the most important roles of the spine is to support the arms. Take time before you begin practicing to feel this in your body as you breathe. Be aware also of the suspension of your arm structure, floating over your ribs via the intricate system of connective tissue covering the muscles and bones. You do not need to hold yourself up or hold your arms up in any way. When you rest your hands on the piano, the piano supports the weight of your arm and you do not need to hold at the elbow.

When dropping the forearm from the elbow for chords and octaves, do not set a position in your hand. Let the piano open your hand to the desired configuration for each chord or octave. This is a more passive opening that avoids overstretching and co-contraction of opposing muscles in the palm. To experience a passive, gentle opening of the hand, place one hand on a table and use the other to open the spaces between the fingers. Remember that the hand opens from the joints where the finger bones meet the wrist bones and from the large knuckle joints. The hand opens like a fan. Access the maximum amount of space between each finger without feeling stretched. The fingers, hand, and arm drop as a unit without any presetting of a hand position. Setting or fixing the hand while dropping or moving from place to place creates tension in the muscles of the forearm.

When you land at the bottom of the keys, there is no collapse of the wrist. The landing is an exact place of balance, differing slightly for each combination of fingers and black and white notes. Using your kinesthetic sense and accessing feedback from those receptors in your wrist and forearm, you can determine where the best height is for each chord or octave. The maximum range of hand opening usually requires a somewhat lower wrist position. Pianists with small hands will use a lower wrist position for octaves than those with larger hands. In general, the wrist position is slightly higher for octaves and chords than for single notes.

Unless you have a large hand, it is best to use fingers 1 and 5 for octaves. Playing octaves with fingers 1 and 4 causes ulnar deviation that can be painful and injurious. By incorporating pedal, tone, and shaping, you can create a musical legato that will simulate the physical connection achieved with 1-4 and 1-5 octaves. Your sound will improve, as you will have less tension in your forearm from the stretching and twisting required for the 1-4 octaves.

Movement from chord to chord or octave to octave is a rebound off the bottom of the key, not a lifting up. In fact, the rebound from each keybed takes you sideways to the next place. As you move across the keyboard, rebounding from place to place, your spine adjusts to the new position, led by your head.

When playing octave passages on black and white keys, there are several things to keep in mind. The relationship of the hand and arm differs slightly for black and white key octaves. Because the black keys are higher in space, our hand is more level with the arm when playing the black key octaves. The white key octaves require the hand to be tilted down slightly in relationship to the arm. Passages with combinations of black and white key octaves also require that you minimize the in and out movements for speed and fluidity. You will notice wrist movement as you play these passages, but be aware that the movement from the keys sequences up the entire arm and that all of the arm joints must be free to move.

Chapter 16
Interpreting Notation

When we rigidly adhere to notation without consideration of the resulting sound or effect on our bodies, we are enslaved to notation. This can result in muscular fatigue and strain and often a less-than-desirable sound. Effective practicing begins with an aural imagination of the desired sound. Discovering the movements to create the desired sound is the next step. Finally, we repeat those chosen movements to reinforce the choreography. This process can be hampered if we do not carefully interpret the marks on the score.

Example 16.1, Schumann's *Papillons*, demonstrates the impossibility of holding long melody tones over an inner voice. If you try to hold the melody tones and stretch to the inner line, you will strain your hand and make it impossible to voice the top line. The solution is to use the pedal, allowing your hand to release from the melody tone and move to the inner voice. As the pedal keeps the melody ringing, you can control the expression of the inner line with the full attention of your arm and finger, slowing the key descent to make a softer sound. By using combinations of over and under shapes, you can move smoothly from voice to voice, allowing the movement of the arm to release your hand and finger to the next place.

Example 16.1. Schumann: *Papillons,* Op. 2, No. 7

Example 16.2, Schubert's Impromptu No. 3 in G-flat Major, is another instance demonstrating the need to let go of the long melody tone to facilitate a lighter touch in the inner arpeggios. It is difficult and unnecessary to require two actions simultaneously in the right hand: holding the melody tone and playing the inner voice lightly. Instead, use the pedal to hold the long melody tones and shaping to move you down for the inner arpeggios. You can create a legato connection from the last eighth note of the fourth beat in the inner voice to the next melody tone on beat five. Creating a physical legato when possible reinforces the musical legato created by the pedal.

Example 16.2. Schubert: Impromptu No. 3 in G-flat Major, Op. 90

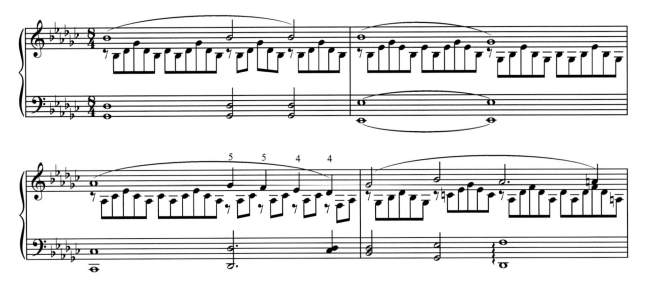

In Example 16.3, the opening of Schubert's Sonata in B-flat Major, we discover an instance where it is impossible to hold the bass line quarter notes for their full value while playing eighth notes in the same hand for the tenor voice. Rotation to the thumb for the second eighth note of each beat releases the bass note slightly early and allows the arm to prepare for the next interval. By using pedal and voicing in the bass line we give the illusion of connection. The speed of the key descent is a mechanism that changes the dynamic level. Thus, voicing is an imperceptibly faster descent of the desired keys, making those notes louder than the other voices. I say imperceptible because this variance should not affect the impression of the listener that both notes are sounding together. An easy way to achieve voicing is to listen more to the voice you wish to bring out; the listener hears what you hear! Also, if you brighten your tactile awareness of the finger, you can better control the release of weight and energy. Often the prominent voice has more inflection and expression than subsidiary voices. Make the voice you wish to be in the foreground the most beautiful. Don't be limited by always bringing out the top voice. Inner voices and bass lines can add orchestral color to your playing when they are highlighted.

Example 16.3. Schubert: Sonata in B-flat Major, Op. posth., 1st movt.

Often a composer writes something that is difficult or impossible for the pianist to play without strain. Keep in mind that all hands are different sizes and shapes and also that the keyboards of the eighteenth and nineteenth centuries were quite different than the modern piano. Bach's fugues were written for the harpsichord, an instrument with very narrow keys and a very light action. The early fortepiano in Beethoven's time had slightly narrower keys, a lighter action, and a pronounced variety in timbre for each register. It was much easier to connect all the voices of the fugues and play the fast octave passages on these earlier instruments. Even Chopin's piano had less metal and more wood than the modern piano, requiring careful interpretation of his pedaling marks. We cannot be enslaved to his pedaling marks, as they were not intended for the modern piano. When a passage appears to be too difficult to play without strain, get creative. Example 16.4, Schumann's "Aufschwung" from *Fantasiestücke*, affords an opportunity to redistribute notes written for the right hand to the left hand in measures 2 and 3. By using a flutter pedal, you can keep the long bass octave ringing while articulating the inner melody with the left hand.

Example 16.4. Schumann: *Fantasiestücke*, Op. 12, No. 2 ("Aufschwung")

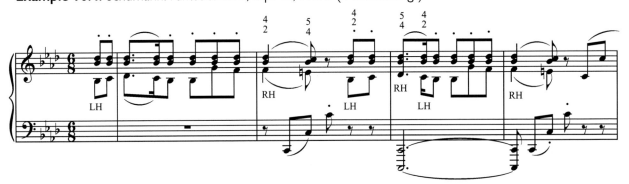

Example 16.5, Schubert's *Moment Musical in A-flat Major*, demonstrates the need to use the pedal to sustain long notes while you move ahead to the next place. By pedaling each dotted half note, you can rebound to the next chord, getting the weight and energy of the arm over it to control the key descent. As you hear the decay of the long note you have left early, you can match that decay with the next

melody note. Creating a legato, singing line is dependent on this skill. If you hold the long note for its full value you will need to move very quickly to the next chord and will not be able to move slowly into the key to create the softer sound you desire for matching the decay of the long note.

Example 16.5. Schubert: Moment Musical in A-flat Major, Op. 94, No. 2

Another skill needed to create the long singing line is the realization that the energy of the arm, potential or kinetic, does not stop until the piece is over. Thus, the half notes in Example 16.6, Chopin's Mazurka in A Minor, are places that the arm moves through via specific shaping to the next note. There is no stopping on the bottom of the keys! I call this skill the "singing arm." As you become aware of the potential and actual movement, or energy, in your arm, you can imagine the sound and rhythm moving through your arm into the keys. Part of this concept is metaphorical, but bear with me. It is, after all, through movement and touch that we translate our aural imagination and emotion into sound at the piano. Thus, do not be restricted by the full value of each note. Use pedal, shaping, and tone to carry your arm through each note to the next place.

Example 16.6. Chopin: Mazurka in A Minor, Op. 17, No. 4

Becoming free to interpret notation is often related to understanding the difference between physical and musical legato. Physical legato is one that implies an actual physical connection between notes with the fingers. This is not always possible, so fortunately we have musical legato to help us. Musical legato incorporates pedal, shaping, and tone. A good application of musical legato is found in Example 16.7, Schumann's *Kreisleriana*. First of all, if your hand is strained by using 1 and 4 for octaves, don't do it. You can play every octave in the melody with fingers 1 and 5 and create a legato effect using the pedal to connect the sounds. Smooth lateral arm movements and varying wrist and arm heights for black and white key octaves, as described in Chapter 14 (Shaping) and Chapter 15 (Octaves and Chords), support the legato line. By being aware of the equality in the timing of depression and release of each octave and aiming your weight and energy to the point of sound, you will create a ringing tone that will sustain the sound of these octaves. The point of sound is that place in the key descent where the hammer is released to strike the string. It is about two-thirds of the way down the depth of the key. Sound is produced here, not at the bottom of the key. By aiming weight and energy to the point of sound, we release the hammer in such a way that more overtones can be produced. Listen to the sound after you play, between the notes, to hear these ringing overtones. Allow each octave to rebound you sideways to the next, creating a forward direction physically through the passage.

Example 16.7. Schumann: *Kreisleriana*, Op. 16, 2nd movt.

When it is not possible to physically connect intervals, you can connect any two notes between consecutive intervals to achieve a legato effect. Chopin's Nocturne in E Minor, Example 16.8, gives an opportunity to apply this principle. In the fourth and fifth measures of the example, there are thirds that cannot all be connected physically. Using fingers 5-3, 4-2, 3-1, and 2-1 for the thirds in measure 4, and then fingers 4-2 in measure 5, you will find it possible to physically connect the thirds between the last two measures. Hold the thumb on the last third of the fourth measure to connect it to fingers 4 and 2 on the downbeat of measure 5. This subtle connection creates a legato effect.

Example 16.8. Chopin: Nocturne in E Minor, Op. 72, No. 1

Another cause for consideration in interpretation is the possibility of a few chords being just too big or strenuous for your hand. I may be treading on thin ice here, but I believe it is allowable to reduce a few chords in order to play a piece comfortably. With all due respect to the composers, I believe most of them want their music played through history and don't want pianists getting hurt. If removing a few notes allows you to play the piece without strain or injury, be respectful and creative in your reductions. Sometimes the note can be taken with another hand in another voice. Often the chord can be rolled to avoid stretching. Sometimes you can just leave out notes, as in Example 16.9, Debussy's "Hommage à Rameau" from *Images (Book I)*. In the fifth measure, I leave the lower A out of the right hand chords at the beginning of the second and third beats. By using the sostenuto pedal at the beginning of this measure, I collect overtones that fill in for this note. Also, the left hand is playing an A one octave lower, so this is a doubled note. The effect is not much different than what is written, and I think it sounds better than rolling those chords. Also, my hand is free of tension from overstretching and I can create a more beautiful tone.

Example 16.9. Debussy: "Hommage à Rameau" from *Images (Book I)*

Finally, do not be limited by an editor's fingering. It is true that they probably have more experience with fingering than you do, but is their hand the same size as yours? Try the fingering suggested by the editor, and if it does not work for you, change it! Keep in mind that many editors choose fingering for a musical effect. Determine what that effect might be, and discover how a better fingering for your hand can achieve this.

It is not necessary to suffer or struggle to play the great piano repertoire. Certainly, we are all aware of the dedication and commitment necessary to achieve our highest goals as pianists. However, I believe strongly that we must let go of historical myths that enslave us to injurious notation and prevent us from creatively expressing ourselves. If classical music is to survive and thrive in the coming centuries, we must explore an open and humane approach, which will make the study of music more accessible and enjoyable.

Chapter 17
Grouping

G rouping is a way of organizing notes conceptually and physically in order to divide a passage into manageable parts. It was first described by Dorothy Taubman and developed extensively at the Taubman Institute. In this chapter we will explore grouping through the use of musical examples that demonstrate various grouping techniques.

Examples 17.1, 17.2, and 17.3 show how to group a passage from a more dense texture to a less dense texture. Playing a chord or interval requires that more weight and energy be delivered through the fingers than for a single note. Thus, when possible, grouping from a chord or interval makes the passage flow more easily. The initial chord or interval feels like a starting impulse for the rest of the notes that then feel part of a unified gesture.

Example 17.1. Chopin: Ballade No. 1 in G Minor, Op. 23   Grouping from Chord

Example 17.2. Chopin: Scherzo No. 3 in C-sharp Minor, Op. 39 — Grouping from Chord

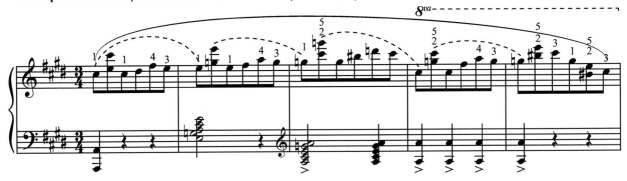

Example 17.3. "Vallée d'Obermann" from *Années de pèlerinage* — Grouping from Chord

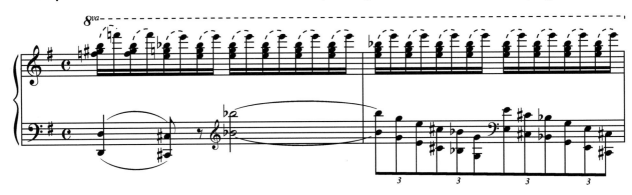

Examples 17.4 and 17.5 show grouping in varying arm positions, or physical neighborhoods. In these examples the group often begins on a single note and moves to an interval. It is more important here to group according to the location of the arm than for the density of the texture. Each group contains notes that can be played with the arm in one location; then the arm moves for the next group.

Example 17.4. Chopin: Scherzo No. 1 in B Minor, Op. 20   Grouping in Physical Neighborhoods

Example 17.5. Chopin: Ballade No. 4 in F Minor, Op. 52   Grouping in Physical Neighborhoods

One of the most helpful applications for grouping is found in Examples 17.6 and 17.7. When notes traveling in the same direction are grouped together, the passage flows physically and musically. Often these physical groups for direction move over the beat and over the bar. If either of these examples were grouped according to the beat, there would be a feeling of excessive movement in two directions. Try the examples both ways and feel the difference.

Example 17.6. Beethoven: 32 Variations in C Minor, var. 21   Grouping for Direction

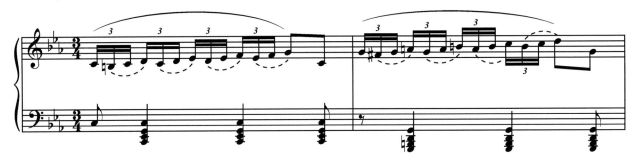

Example 17.7. Mendelssohn: *Songs Without Words*, Op. 67, No. 4   Grouping for Direction
     ("Spinning Song")

Stretching is a common problem pianists encounter, and it is best to avoid opening the hand beyond the mid-range when possible. Grouping to avoid stretching is found in Examples 17.8 and 17.9. In Example 17.8, the group extends over two beats and begins with a smaller interval expanding to an octave. In Example 17.9, the left hand and arm rotate up toward the thumb for each new group, avoiding stretching between fingers 5 and 4.

Example 17.8. Chopin: *Fantaisie-Impromptu*, Op. 66   Grouping to Avoid Stretching

Example 17.9. Chopin: Ballade No. 1 in G Minor, Op. 23   Grouping to Avoid Stretching

In Example 17.10, the Schubert Sonata in A Minor, Op. 143, we find a grouping from quick note to long note. It is difficult to move to and away from a note quickly. If you group the short note (sixteenth note) with the long note (dotted eighth note) and use the pedal to sustain the long note, you can move ahead to each new group. You can actually be over the new group before you play down by using the pedal to sustain the sound. Feeling the short note movement to the long note also clarifies the dotted rhythm.

Example 17.10. Schubert: Sonata in A Minor, Op. 143, 1st movt.   Grouping from Quick Note

The last category of grouping, according to the beat, is probably the most familiar. We use this often to underscore the pulse, and when the passage is designed to fit this metric grouping, the rhythm and physical grouping intersect. In Examples 17.11 and 17.12 the grouping occurs around the half note and dotted half note, respectively.

Example 17.11. Mozart: Sonata in C Major, K. 545, 1st movt.   Grouping According to Beat

Example 17.12. Chopin: Ballade No. 1 in G Minor, Op. 23   Grouping According to Beat

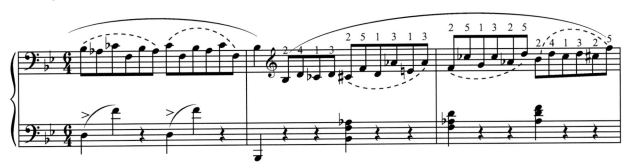

Chapter 18
Choreography of the Hands

Choreography of the hands organizes the playing of the right and left hands so that the kinesthetic experience is unified. The examples included in this chapter demonstrate various challenges for movements between the hands.

When alternating the hands as in the example *Asturias (Leyenda)* by Albéniz, it is important to have a sense of "cueing" from one hand to the other. This can be likened to when a ball or baton is passed off in a relay. You feel the weight and energy moving smoothly from the right hand to the left hand and then from the left hand back to the right. Careful attention to rebound off the bottom of the key for the staccato articulation required in this passage helps the evenness of the alternating hands.

Example 18.1. Albéniz: "Asturias (Leyenda)" from *Suite Espagnole*, Op. 47, No. 5   Alternating Hands

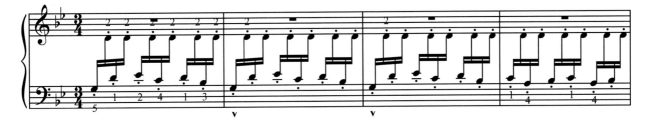

For polyrhythm, as in Example 18.2, interdependence can be likened to a mathematical equation. You can clearly delineate where the two rhythms intersect and measure the distance between notes that do not. For the three-against-four polyrhythm shown in this example, use the common denominator of these two numbers, which is twelve. Graph the two rhythms along the twelve-note continuum to see where they intersect. This process is shown below the example. Later it is best to feel the composite rhythm as one kinesthetic, unified experience. Methods to achieve this are described in Chapter 20 (Internalizing Rhythm).

Example 18.2. Beethoven: Sonata in G Major, Op. 79, 3rd movt.   Polyrhythms

When ornaments or broken chords appear in the music, it is important to determine their timing. The Mozart Sonata in A Major, K. 331, Example 18.3, contains a passage in the third movement requiring this analysis. The three grace notes in the left hand can be played immediately after the last sixteenth note of the right hand to ensure that the rhythm is not disturbed. In the next example, Chopin's Ballade No. 1 in G Minor, Op. 23, we find an example of how timing of the rolled chord in the left hand ensures that the right hand interval lands together with the top note of the left hand chord.

Example 18.3. Mozart: Sonata in A Major, K. 331, 3rd movt.   Broken Chords and Ornaments

Example 18.4. Chopin: Ballade No. 1 in G Minor, Op. 23   Broken Chords and Ornaments

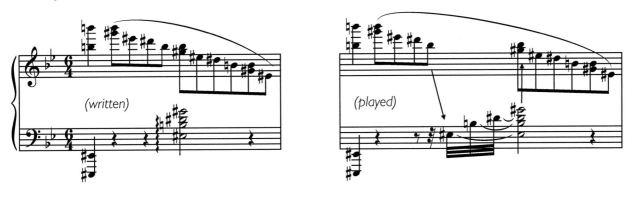

Often the musical elements of legato and staccato occur at the same time, requiring a different touch in each hand. If you can separate the feeling of each hand, you will be able to achieve this more easily. The Haydn sonata in Example 18.5 requires the right hand to play legato sixteenth notes and the left hand to play staccato eighth notes. The right hand will feel a connection from key bottom to key bottom to create a physical legato. The left hand will access rebound off the bottom of the key, a feeling of light bouncing, to achieve the staccato effect. Allow the two hands to feel different and notice this difference.

Example 18.5. Haydn: Sonata in E-flat Major, Hob. XVI:52, 3rd movt. Legato Against Stacato

Voicing is one of the most important musical elements pianists can access to convey the beauty of melodic lines and to add color to their sound. Many theories about how to achieve voicing have been presented over time in the piano pedagogy literature. The theory for voicing that I have found to be the most successful and least injurious is based on the physical properties of sound production at the piano. When we voice a note, we make it louder and more prominent. Dynamics on the piano are affected by the speed of the key descent and, to some extent, the mass used to depress the key. One way to achieve voicing is to feel the finger playing the important notes more brightly in your tactile awareness. If you also hear these melody notes more prominently, your body will respond by delivering more weight and energy to those voiced notes. Sometimes the metaphor of delivering more weight to the melody fingers and feeling the accompaniment fingers as lighter is also helpful. This is a metaphor, as we cannot change the weight of our fingers! Example 18.6 provides the opportunity to experiment with voicing of the top notes in the right hand as well as the inner melody of the left hand.

Example 18.6. Grieg: *Lyric Pieces*, Op. 57, No. 1 ("Vanished Days") Voicing

When the hands leap at the same time, it is important to determine which hand will lead. The brain cannot process both hands moving at exactly the same time, so establishing a leader will ensure a smooth leap. In Example 18.7, from Schumann's *Kreisleriana*, both hands leap down every two bars. In this case, as the leaps are a similar distance and in the same direction, the left hand leads. Variables to consider when determining the leading hand for a leap include the distance of each leap, as you might want to move the hand with the largest distance first, and the direction of the leap, since if both hands move in the same direction one hand will need to get out of the way for the other hand to move. Example 18.8, from Ginastera's Piano Sonata No. 1, Op. 22, requires this choreography to navigate larger leaps. In bar 5 both hands leap down, so the left hand leads. Both hands then leap up in this measure, so the right hand leads. If the hands are leaping in opposite directions, usually the hand with the larger leap will lead the movement.

Example 18.7. Schumann: *Kreisleriana*, Op. 16   Leaps

Example 18.8. Ginastera: Piano Sonata No. 1, Op. 22, 1st movt.   Leaps

Understanding choreography of the hands is also important for memory work. Analysis and listening to composite intervals between the hands reinforces aural memory. Noticing and naming the distance between the hands reinforces kinesthetic memory, and awareness of which fingers in each hand play together enhances tactile memory. To test this last concept, play an A major scale with both hands and notice that your third fingers always play together.

When the hands are required to play over each other, there are two ways to create space. The first dimension is between the heights of each hand—one hand can play lower and the other hand higher. Combine this with one hand playing more "in" toward the fallboard and the other playing more "out" toward your body and you will have accessed the most available space between the hands. Usually the hand that plays lower is also out near the edge of the key. The other hand plays in and higher.

The hands can teach each other new habits! Let's say your right hand has a habit of curling the little finger and the left hand does not. By accessing the kinesthetic sense of your left hand, you may be able to release the muscles and tendons that have a habit of over-flexing your right little finger. In order to accomplish this you must feel your left hand fully, maybe even with your eyes closed, then match that feeling in the right hand.

Chapter 19
Learning and Memorizing

Each person must develop their own system of learning and memorizing music based on their learning style and the type of music that they are studying. Effective systems accelerate the learning process and yield solid memorization, reducing performance anxiety related to fear of memory slips. The following outline details my current method of learning and memorizing. This formula has evolved over my forty years of piano study. For many years I had no system other than playing a piece over and over until my muscle memory was secure. Obviously, this was inefficient and incomplete. As you review my system, keep in mind that you will want to develop your own unique method of learning and memorizing that is creative and enjoyable. Then, of course, you must follow it and let it evolve as you discover more about how your brain works.

1. Sight-read and/or listen to a recording of the piece to determine if you really love it and want to work on it. There are literally thousands of piano pieces in our literature. Challenge yourself to become familiar with different composers and styles and to seek the appropriate pieces that speak to you as a musician and artist. Even within the constraints of music school requirements, there is room for exploration of the literature to find the right piece for you. Be proactive and participatory in the repertoire selection process.

2. Analyze the large-scale form of the piece, making notations on the score. Complete a harmonic analysis of the piece.

3. For any given practice session, determine which section you are going to work on for that period of time. If you are planning to memorize the piece, begin memory work immediately.

4. Establish a good fingering for the section you are working on. Write in any fingering that differs from the editor's or that you might forget. Remember, most editors are men with large hands. If you have small hands, you very well may discover a better fingering for your hand. Always try the editor's fingering first. If it is uncomfortable or unworkable, by all means change it!

5. Do a phrase analysis of the section you are working on. Mark the phrases in the music and determine the highpoints or climaxes of each phrase. Elements of the music that give clues to highpoints are: register, dynamics, articulation, meter placement, underlying harmony, and the rhythmic value of notes.

6. If you plan to memorize the piece, begin working phrase by phrase, following the steps below. Keep in mind an understanding of what practicing is—not finding the notes, but rather discovering the movements that create the sound you want.

    a. Memorize hands separately.
    b. Play from memory with counting.
    c. Play from memory chanting harmony.
    d. Play from memory singing the melody.
    e. Play from memory attending to all of the musical elements.
    f. Play from memory with awareness focused on freedom of movement.
    g. Close your eyes and run the phrase in your sensory imagination: hearing, seeing, and feeling every aspect of the phrase in your mind. Most pianists see the geography of the keyboard in their visual imagination; some see the score. The keyboard is a closer representation of the reality of what you are touching to create sound. **Note:** You will need to play the phrase with the score and refer to the score often during this process.

7. Alternate memory work with careful play-throughs of the piece using the score. Discover the choreography of movement needed for the sound you desire. Work at a tempo that allows for detailed study and freedom of movement. Speed is a later step in the process of learning and should never undermine the initial steps.

In order to maintain a balanced and enjoyable practice routine, I intersperse my memory work of new pieces with several other activities. These include playing through pieces in my performance repertoire, working on skills and sight-reading, improvising, composing, working on literature I am not planning to memorize, and playing fun, easy pieces.

Memory work is a continuous process. The following is a list of helpful ways to keep your memory of a piece bright in your mind:

1. Review all of the initial memory steps often.
2. Ask yourself: "What don't I know about this passage or phrase?"
3. Play phrases with eyes closed to heighten kinesthetic, tactile, and aural senses.
4. Mark phrases (touch keys without depressing) to heighten visual and tactile senses.
5. Play the piece backwards phrase by phrase to eliminate contextual learning.
6. Include performances for yourself and friends where you cannot stop and must improvise through memory slips.
7. Keep pieces in your repertoire for a long time and perform them often.
8. Run the entire piece, even entire program, in your sensory imagination. Review any passages at the keyboard that you cannot clearly imagine.

Chapter 20
Internalizing Rhythm

Rhythm is defined as everything pertaining to the duration of musical sound. Our awareness of this musical element is housed in our kinesthetic sense, and rhythm determines the timing of all of our movements. Everyone who has danced, tapped their feet, or clapped their hands in time to music has experienced this marriage of movement and rhythm. In order to understand rhythm and incorporate this in our practicing and performing, we must internalize the rhythm—in other words, feel it in our bodies. There are several aspects of rhythm that can be internalized and several methods of going about this process. We shall explore metrical rhythm, beat, harmonic rhythm, polyrhythm, and the use of the metronome in this chapter. Methods to experience and expand awareness of rhythm will also be discovered.

Metrical rhythm refers to the unit each measure creates in a given time signature and the beat and metric accents within it. For example, in 4/4 time, the beat is a quarter note and the metric accents are stronger on the first beat and weaker on the third beat of each measure. To internalize the metric rhythm, you can conduct your piece from the score while hearing the music in your aural imagination, singing the melody, or listening to a recording. Conducting uses larger muscle groups and simplifies the neuromuscular task considerably from the actual playing of the piece. The beat and metric rhythm become more prominent in your sensory awareness through this activity. Another fun way to internalize the metric rhythm and beat of your piece is to put on a recording and dance to the music. Adding clapping or clicking of your fingers will enhance the experience of syncopations and subdivisions. If you are working on memorization, you can hear your piece in your aural imagination as you walk or run, solidifying the tempo and consistency of your rhythm as you choose your running or walking pace. One of the best ways to learn the rhythm of your piece is to tap the rhythm with both hands on the key cover while counting. This exercise gives you a consistent pulse and a kinesthetic awareness of the interdependence of the subdivisions in each hand. In other words, you feel how the rhythms of each hand come together to form one kinesthetic experience. It's easier to feel the rhythm this way without having to worry about playing all of the notes.

Harmonic rhythm is the rhythmic movement contributed to music by the underlying changes of harmony. These combine with and support the metric rhythm. To experience the harmonic rhythm, you must first do a harmonic analysis of your piece and begin to hear harmonically. This can be accomplished by singing the bass line with chord functions. Later you can "sing the counts," identifying the beats on which harmonic movement of the bass line occurs. Simplifying the chords and playing them as a chord progression while counting aloud will also contribute to your understanding of harmonic rhythm.

The simultaneous use of two or more rhythms is termed *polyrhythm.* Polyrhythms can be challenging if your only tool for understanding is a mathematical equation of the intersection of two subdivisions. Although it may be helpful to know where the intersection of notes in a two-against-three pattern occurs, it is easier to feel the composite rhythm in your body. To experience a two-against-three polyrhythm, begin by stepping the larger beats and counting aloud. Then you can add tapping both hands on your thighs with the duple subdivision. The last step would be to add the triplet figure against the duple figure with one of your hands. This exercise can be adapted for any polyrhythm.

One of the most helpful systems for understanding polyrhythm is TaKeTiNa. This rhythm training incorporates stepping, clapping, vocalizing, and the playing of instruments to internalize rhythm and polyrhythm. The process, developed by Austrian percussionist Reinhard Flatischler, provides a musical, meditative group experience for people who want to develop their awareness of rhythm. TaKeTiNa sessions are offered internationally by trained teachers.

The metronome is a helpful tool for establishing tempo and maintaining consistency of the pulse. It is, however, an external agent—not linked directly to our kinesthetic sense. It is much better to establish the habit of counting aloud as you learn a piece to clearly link vocalization with your sense of pulse. Counting also aids memorization, as it identifies when events occur in each measure. The metronome can also be used as a guide to developing a reliable internal sense of tempo. Challenge yourself to count or conduct the tempo you desire and then check to see how close you are with the metronome. Internal sense of tempo is an acquired skill and can be developed if you use the metronome to check rather than to dictate. Of course, if you are having trouble keeping a strict tempo, the metronome is an indispensable reminder of a steady beat. A creative way to solidify your tempo is to place the metronome on the off beats. This "reggae" metronome clearly identifies when you are short-changing weaker beats such as beats two and four in a 4/4 meter, which often happens. To experience the "reggae" metronome in a 4/4 meter, set it to a half note value and have the second and fourth beats line up with the clicks. A drum machine or rhythm setting on an electronic keyboard can also be used as a metronome.

Collaborative activities to solidify rhythm are very effective and enjoyable. Ask a friend to clap or play rhythm instruments while you practice. If you are lucky enough to know a good drummer, practice with them and allow your sense of pulse to mesh with theirs. As a teacher, you can gently tap on the shoulders of your students to help them feel the pulse in their bodies.

Finally, any activity that enhances your sense of rhythm should be explored as much as possible. If you think you have two left feet, take a dance class! Remember that the brain is plastic and can create new neuronal pathways at any time. Consider learning to conduct or studying TaKeTiNa. Dalcroze eurhythmics is also a powerful tool for learning about rhythm through movement, with classes and workshops offered nationwide. Pick up a percussion instrument and play along with the music, or better yet, build a percussion instrument collection to hand out at parties so everyone can play along with the music. Rhythm is the fundamental basis of all music and was also probably the first expression of music in human culture. The stronger your internal sense of rhythm, the more you will have to offer as a performer and teacher.

Chapter 21
Moving Into Speed

The first step to playing fast with freedom and confidence is to examine your initial learning process. Each piece should be carefully studied and worked out at a manageable tempo before increasing speed. Intend to learn notes, rhythm, fingering, and musical elements without tension or anxious thoughts. Keep your kinesthetic sense bright in your awareness as you learn, noticing and eliminating unnecessary muscular tension or awkward movements. Carefully choreograph difficult passages from the beginning of the learning process. Many times we set ourselves up for obstacles by carrying on a conversation in our minds with thoughts like: "I'll never get this up to tempo," or " I can't play as fast as the great pianists." Be aware of these thoughts and surround them with positive ideas, such as "I know I can play fast, because I play my scales fast," and "I have a plan for increasing speed that will work for me," or "I will get the tempo as fast as I can for now and that will be my expression of the piece." It is helpful to have a "target tempo" for each piece. This tempo reflects the composer's intentions, your personal expression of the piece, and your technical ability at the time. It is wise to choose pieces in which these three considerations can enhance each other.

After learning the piece so you can play it easily at a slow tempo, you can begin to plan your practice around increasing speed. There are several valid approaches to this process that may be more suitable to individual pianists or certain pieces. The more strategies you have at your fingertips, the more successful you will be in achieving your goal of playing fast with freedom.

The simplest way to increase speed in practicing is to "notch up" the metronome. Let's say you can play your piece at 88 to the quarter note. You could increase the tempo one notch at a time—being sure not to move ahead until the entire piece feels comfortable at the new tempo.

Another strategy is to play small portions, perhaps two- to four-measure units, at the target tempo. It is helpful to pause often when practicing this way to release tension in your arms. This can be done simply by letting your arms rest at your sides, allowing gravity to release any holding in the elbow or forearm muscles. After you can play a few small units at the target tempo, you can put them together to form larger, faster units.

Playing phrases hands separately at faster tempos is a great strategy to reinforce kinesthetic and tactile awareness. Usually one hand "knows" the passage better than the other. Any insecurity makes it difficult to move into speed.

Practicing in rhythms is an effective way to alternate the speed between notes. Use a dotted rhythm "long-short" and "short-long" for divisions of two notes and "long-short-short," "short-long-short," and "short-short-long" for triplets. Be sure to play all combinations of the rhythm for each passage.

Grouping notes into gestures is a very important element of moving into speed. The brain can more easily grasp a unit of movement that includes several notes rather than each individual note in a fast passage. Often the grouping is reinforced by kinesthetic awareness of the physical shape of the passage. When grouping notes together, the larger curvilinear movement of the arm is most bright in your awareness, although you still feel your fingers moving and playing each key.

A corollary to the concept of grouping is the concept of a start note that begins the impulse for the group. Usually this "start" has more energy delivered from the arm and the following notes feel as if they are a result of the first initial impulse. A metaphor for this concept would be a rock skipping across the water. The first time it hits the water there is more energy transmitted. The following skips are like rebounds of the first.

Practicing with a larger rhythmic unit in mind aids fast playing. Often you can count measures of a phrase or even two-bar units. This is, in effect, a rhythmic grouping which gives the mind and body a larger unit to comprehend.

Here are some helpful concepts to keep in mind as you experiment with moving into speed:

1. Never sacrifice clarity or musical expression for speed.

2. Be vigilant in your awareness of mental and physical tension; scan your body from head to toe as you play fast to discover unnecessary tension.

3. Practice playing scales and arpeggios fast.

4. Remember that moving into speed may mean minimizing larger arm and torso movements and incorporating more finger movement.

5. Explore how much effort is required to play a passage faster. Moving faster does not always mean more work. As with walking and running, if your body is trained and free of tension, moving from walking to running is a natural, easy flow.

6. Don't try to play fast with cold hands or a cold body. Use a heating pad, warm water, or do some aerobic exercise to get your blood circulating before you practice.

7. Slow your mind as you practice fast. Focus on larger, more inclusive concepts such as breathing, spinal support, and contact with the three solid surfaces (the keybed, bench, and floor).

8. Alternate practicing slow and fast pieces.

9. Don't become trapped by editorial metronome markings or recordings. These tempos often reflect the editor's opinion. Even a composer's metronome marking may be misleading if it applies to an instrument that differs from the modern piano. Chopin's and Beethoven's pianos had a much lighter action. Thus, playing fast was easier! Your target tempo should reflect your knowledge of the composer's intentions, your personal interpretation, and your present technical ability.

10. The longer you keep a piece in your repertoire, the easier it is to play fast. You may even be able to continually increase the tempo of that piece, up to a point.

11. Each practice session will yield a finite amount of progress in increasing the tempo. When you reach the point of diminishing returns for your efforts, it is best to take a break and return to the process at another time. Often we need to remain at one tempo plateau for a period of time before our body is ready to move faster.

Part III
Wellness Principles

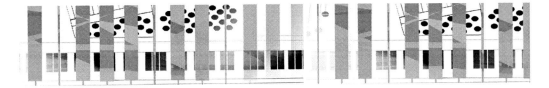

Chapter 22
The Self Map

The self map refers to our internal impressions of who we are. For musicians this includes who we are in every aspect of our profession: practicing, performing, collaborating, creating, and teaching. We are musicians in a broad sense that encompasses our instrument and our artistry. To begin exploring this concept, a few terms must be defined. What is an artist, musician, and pianist? The definition of artist is broad and covers a number of activities having to do with creating art, practicing art, or demonstrating art. A musician is someone who plays or writes music, and a pianist is a musician who plays the piano. If we accept these simple definitions, it will be easier to create an identity for ourselves within the musical and artistic communities. Identities do not necessarily imply egotism, although the ego is involved in the identity. When exploring our self-perception, or self map, it is important to be realistic, humble, and flexible. We can see ourselves as we are now while rationally setting future goals. We can be honest about our attributes while acknowledging the talents and contributions of other musicians.

In the book *Performing Music in the Age of Recording* (2004), Robert Philip brings a number of pitfalls common to the identities of modern musicians to light. Perfectionism has become a goal for many of us due to the artificial nature of perfect recordings. Instead of seeking the perfect connection with our music and audience, we strive for note perfection. Is this really an artistic goal? According to one of Beethoven's students, the master was forgiving of a few missed notes but furious when expression was sacrificed.[6] Certainly playing the notes the composer wrote

---

6. Reginald R. Gerig, *Famous Pianists and Their Techniques*, 2nd ed. (Bloomington: Indiana University Press, 2007), 90.

is important. However, if this becomes your ultimate goal, the means with which you proceed will be sterile and empty. Using inclusive awareness, it is possible to include playing the right notes with all of the interpretive elements of the score, while exploring the expression of the piece and what it means to you. After all, music is the communication of ideas and emotions, not just hammering out a string of predetermined, rigid sounds.

Before recordings became the predominant form of musical communication, musicians in different parts of the world had vastly different interpretations of the same piece. Now we have certain accepted high standards from gifted performers to which we aspire. Take, for example, the celebrated recordings of the Chopin Etudes by Murray Perahia. The depth of expression and breathtaking tempos displayed by this great artist captivate pianists around the world. Listening to his recording will give students many wonderful ideas for their own performances. But is it realistic or desirable to strive for mimicry of this recording? Would it be more reasonable and enjoyable to find a tempo possible for you, within the range of the composer's tempo marking? Do you have something unique to bring to this piece that is different from Mr. Perahia and reflects your careful interpretation of Chopin's score?

Author Robert Philip also explores the loss of respect for the amateur musician in our modern society. In the nineteenth century, music flourished in most homes, and gatherings of all levels of performers were common. Live music was an important form of social interaction. If you have ever had the pleasure of attending a house concert, you have experienced this unique form of human connection. In this age of extremes, we mistakenly count only concert soloists as artists. What about the church musicians, folk guitarists, and Indian raga ensembles? If we accept the broad definitions of musicians and artists, it is possible to respect many types of music from diverse sources. It is also easier to define our own place in the world of music using the concept of the self map.

Self maps include many aspects. They reflect our education, current employment, professional goals, musical affinities, and our highest dreams and aspirations. These maps grow and change as we move along our musical paths. There is no problem with creating and recreating these maps frequently. The loss lies in not being aware of your identity as an artist, musician, or pianist. Without this basic reflection, you cannot successfully communicate through music. Although the ultimate goal of any performance may be to communicate ideas and emotions through sound, without self knowledge we are fooling ourselves and our audience about the source of this communication. Practicing and performing include an awareness of who we are within the community of musicians.

Many students struggle with how to describe themselves and their importance in the world of music. Be assured that this struggle and introspection are essential. When we are fully present in our practice and performances, realistically viewing our abilities and purpose, the music has more meaning.

Questions for Reflection:

1. How do you view yourself as an artist, musician, and pianist?
2. What are your most outrageous professional goals?
3. How have you been affected by the pursuit of perfectionism in your practicing and performing?
4. What is the value of establishing and belonging to a community of musicians?

Chapter 23
The Community of Musicians

As musicians we play a unique role in our society, providing entertainment for every occasion and augmenting the enjoyment of the other arts such as dance and motion pictures. The wide array of musical styles is testimony to the variety of sounds that inspire and evoke emotion in our audiences. Most people love music, and most people have certain music they love. Whether we listen to the blues or Beethoven, through music we connect with the human emotional experience.

This incredible opportunity to reflect and enhance the human experience is one of the reasons we practice and teach hours, days, and years of our lives. Whether we play in a rock band or in the symphony, we are all part of the same community of musicians traveling on the same path. All too often our bond to each other is threatened by competition, one-upmanship, and the perception of scarcity in job opportunities. Through respect and acknowledgment of all musical styles and venues, our community can grow and thrive, providing opportunities for each of our members. In this age of dwindling support and aging audiences for our finest symphony orchestras and concert series, it is imperative that we develop an inclusive community with ties to the next generation. Many younger musicians thrive on developing their musicianship in several genres. By day they attend the music schools, and by night they play in the clubs. This is a necessary financial strategy and also a statement of the open-minded and inclusive attitude they have toward their art form.

By examining a few myths about success in music we can begin to foster a supportive environment for all of the musicians in our communities. It surprised me to hear that some of the talented and dedicated jazz pianists at our institution felt second rate to the classical players. True, there is great merit for all musicians in studying the classical repertoire, but on the other hand, shouldn't we all be learning to improvise? In the nineteenth century, pianists were expected to improvise on the spot for social gatherings. Many of the great composers, such as Beethoven and Liszt, improvised on their own pieces as they performed and called upon their improvisations for inspiration while composing. Every style of music played well has merit and purpose in our culture, and many styles offer opportunities for learning and development of musical skills. Realistically, we cannot all become experts in all styles of music. Yet it is important to be aware of the dedication, talent, and contributions of all musicians.

Competitions in the world of classical music are an important tool for encouraging and evaluating excellence. Some students are more inclined to benefit from these events than others, and as teachers this is an important distinction to make. The process of preparing for a competition is part of the winning, in my mind. As we prepare our students for a more critical listening of their performance, we grow as teachers and encourage our students to become more aware of every element of their sound. Whether a pianist wins a competition or not, success has been gained through the careful preparation. I also believe it is important to consider the subjective, or human, element of every competition outcome. If we accept this as part of the process, decisions made by adjudicators will not detract from the learning gained from the experience. Competitions can be viewed as a community celebration of excellence for all the participants, and if competitions are only one part of a musician's musical development, balance will be maintained.

Musical collaborations are extremely important for pianists. We spend so many hours in isolation practicing while our colleagues are in symphony rehearsals with their friends. To my way of thinking, every pianist should cultivate accompanying and chamber music opportunities. When we make music with other musicians, we are expanding our experience to include other members of our community. In a chamber music or accompanying setting, there should be no competition. Instead, we collaborate to express the music together. We learn to listen to each other and make musical decisions collectively. There is a feeling of mutual support, and performing becomes less nerve-racking. Whether the collaboration occurs in our living room or on the concert stage, we have gained access to that special place of connection with other musicians.

Employment opportunities for musicians are a constant source of concern. Many musicians graduate from music schools only to find they cannot support themselves with their acquired skills. Through organizations such as the American Federation of Musicians and the Music Teachers National Association, musicians can unite and network for employment and the sharing of knowledge. These organizations post job opportunities in their publications and allow members to offer their services through webpages and monthly journals. In addition, musicians with a variety of skills and adaptability find it easier to support themselves. Pianists can draw upon their training as performers, accompanists, and teachers to create a financially sound lifestyle. Through networking and referrals, musicians can help each other find musical opportunities that enhance both their own personal lives and their cultural environment.

By developing an inclusive appreciation of all musical styles, balancing competition with collaboration, and networking to expand opportunities, musicians can create a healthy community. Without these tools we are separated and bound to antiquated models that promote isolation, fear, and ignorance. Through awareness and care for our community members we can be assured that music will continue its prominent role as one of the most important elements of human culture.

Questions for Reflection:

1. What unique gifts do you possess as a musician that will contribute to your community?
2. How can you increase your connection with musicians in your community?
3. What possibilities for employment can you discover and share with your fellow musicians?

Chapter 24
Performance Anxiety

The words *performance anxiety* are a familiar part of any Western musician's vocabulary. We have all felt the power of this fear-inducing phrase and sometimes take it for granted that this must be part of being a musician. But is this necessarily true? By examining cultural myths and physiologic facts, we can sort out the real meaning of these words and take control over the bodily responses we have when we perform.

Let's begin with dictionary definitions of these two words. According to the unabridged Webster's dictionary, *performance* is defined as follows: "in performing arts, an event in which one person or group of people (performers) behave in a certain way for another group of people (audience). Usually performers participate in rehearsals ahead of time and usually the audience claps to show appreciation. In Japan silence is the greatest compliment."[7] Using the same source, *anxiety* is defined thusly: "A psychological and physiological state characterized by painful feelings such as anger, fear, apprehension or worry and physical sensations such as heart palpitations, nausea, chest pain, shortness of breath, increased blood pressure and pulse, sweating and dilated pupils."[8] Do these words really compliment each other? Should performing be a "fear-inducing" event? Musicians in other cultures do not think so. Barbara Conable relates the story of an encounter with a great African drummer at a Percussive Arts Society convention. When asked about performance anxiety, he said he had never met anyone who suffered from it. He added, laughing, "We are not afraid of music." What a relief it would be to not

---

7. *Webster's Third New International Dictionary Unabridged*, s.v. "performance."
8. Ibid., s.v. "anxiety."

associate fear with music! Perhaps we could rephrase "performance anxiety" as "performance excitement." The term *excitement* would add significant meaning to our performances, as it is defined as "the act of being called to an activity or roused to an emotional response."[9] A true artist is someone who can express emotions in such a way that it creates emotions in others. If your primary response to making music for others is fear, this is what they will feel.

The symptoms often felt in response to performing are real physiological events. The symptoms of anxiety originate deep in the brain (the brainstem). One key region is the hypothalamus, which coordinates behavior (such as drinking to adjust water volume, or breathing rate and depth), hormonal output, and the autonomic nervous system. The autonomic nervous system consists of the sympathetic and parasympathetic divisions, which in some cases work in opposition and in others synergistically to regulate the internal environment. The sympathetic nervous system acts on the tissues using the neurotransmitter norepinephrine (or noradrenaline) and the hormone epinephrine (or adrenaline). The parasympathetic nervous system utilizes acetylcholine as the neurotransmitter to the target tissues.

These two divisions work in a state of balance to ensure adequate blood supply to the tissues, balance of salt and water, regulation of body temperature, and regulation of other critical variables consistent with health and survival. Depending on the circumstances, one or the other of these divisions may predominate. For example, the activity of the parasympathetic division is enhanced during digestion to increase blood flow, absorption, and motility in the gastrointestinal tract.

Under stressful conditions, the hypothalamus helps to ready the body by promoting the release of the stress hormone cortisol from the adrenal cortex via the pituitary, and increasing the output of the sympathetic division to increase blood and oxygen supply to the brain and skeletal muscle, the so-called "fight-or-flight response." These sympathetic actions include constriction of blood vessels to the gastrointestinal tract, dilation of the airways to the lungs, an increase in the strength and rate of contraction of the heart, and an increase in blood pressure. In addition,

---

9. *Webster's Third New International Dictionary Unabridged*, s.v. "excitement."

sympathetic stimulation leads to pupillary dilation and reduction and thickening of salivary secretion. The rate and depth of breathing are increased by stimulation of the associated neural centers in the lower brainstem that control breathing through the phrenic and intercostal nerves.

On a slower time scale, cortisol promotes the production and release of glucose to fuel the brain and skeletal muscle by breaking down glycogen and protein. Prolonged periods of stress can lead to the wasting of muscle and bone.

The hypothalamus is also connected to areas of the brain that are associated with anxiety, other emotional states, and cognition. Anxiety can lead to increased sympathetic activity through the hypothalamus, and the feelings associated with sympathetic activity can increase anxiety, potentially creating a vicious cycle. In the fight-or-flight response, cognition is also enhanced to help deal with the emergency situation. Therefore, a modest increase in hypothalamic action that enhances sympathetic activity can potentially promote a good performance.

In his book *The Relaxation Response* (2000), Dr. Herbert Benson describes the scientific benefits of relaxation. The Relaxation Response is a helpful way to reduce the fight-or-flight response and bring the body back to pre-stress levels. Dr. Benson describes the Relaxation Response as a physical state of deep relaxation that engages the other part of our nervous system—the parasympathetic nervous system. There are many methods to elicit the Relaxation Response, including visualization, progressive muscle relaxation, energy healing, acupuncture, massage, breathing techniques, prayer, meditation, tai chi, qi gong, and yoga. These techniques can help alleviate the anxiety we may feel before a performance.

As well as practicing relaxation techniques, examine your mindset regarding performing. When practicing, teaching, rehearsing, or performing, remove fear from the equation. Music does not equal fear! As you begin to cultivate a calm and centered approach to your music, you will develop the habit of rest and repose in response to all musical situations. Intend to shift your thoughts and words from fear and judgment to a calm acceptance of the present moment in your music. You can make steady improvement much more enjoyably with this approach.

There is no substitute for preparation in the pursuit of fearless performing. In fact, there is probably great benefit gained from over-preparing. Determine how much time you think you need to prepare for a given performance and add time for reinforcement. Become a fan of slow, careful practice. When speed is brought in too quickly, the sympathetic nervous system may become activated. Part of preparation for any major concert is "practice" performances. Take advantage of friends, relatives, and retirement centers for comfortable performing experiences. If you are not ready for a concert when it approaches, consider canceling, changing the repertoire, or postponing the event if possible.

If you are playing from memory, develop a series of strategies to deepen your memory work and to fall back on in performance. An example of this would be to have many starting places in the music that you can readily jump to. It is also helpful to develop the skill of improvising through a memory slip. Remember that memory work is part of our daily practice and must be reviewed continuously for each piece.

Let go of self-consciousness. Performing is not about you—it is about the music! You are a vehicle for the emotions and ideas you are expressing; let the music flow through you unhampered by too much ego involvement. Learn to take criticism gracefully as information given to you for you to utilize. Try not to let any one person or comment determine who you are as a musician or artist. In other words, don't take it personally.

Just as important as these mind-centering strategies are specific strategies to relax your body as you practice and perform. One of the best ways to calm your body is to pay attention to your breathing. By this I mean to actually feel the movements of breathing as described in this book. Thinking about your breathing and feeling your breathing are two entirely different things. The first involves a thought, and the second involves the reception of information from sensory neurons. When you begin to feel your breathing, it will naturally deepen and slow down. You will relax your mind and body through your breathing.

Steps to elicit the Relaxation Response, adapted from *The Relaxation Response*:

1. Sit quietly in a comfortable position.
2. Close your eyes.
3. Deeply relax all your muscles, beginning at your feet and progressing up to your face. Keep them relaxed.
4. Breathe through your nose. Become aware of your breathing. Breathe easily and naturally.
5. Continue for ten to twenty minutes.

Chapter 25
Handwriting and Computer Use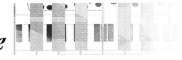

All too often pianists who have retrained their movements at the piano re-injure themselves while handwriting or at the computer. This problem is related to a lack of self-awareness and strong habits acquired through years of experience with these tasks. If you are recovering from an injury, it is wise to cultivate the same level of kinesthetic awareness, or embodiment, as you write and type that you are developing at the piano. Some pianists find great comfort in alternating computer work and handwriting with playing the piano, as they find their inclusive awareness can be more consistently maintained.

If you are experiencing discomfort as you write, become aware of all aspects of this task. Begin with examining your usual writing surface and posture. Ideally, you want to have at least one writing surface that allows your arms to be parallel to the floor and a chair that allows you to sit at balance with your feet on the floor. You can vary your writing positions by using a clipboard and doing some writing while standing at a counter or by your piano. Variation in the approach to any task reduces the risk of repetitive injury and provides opportunity to refresh your inclusive awareness as you change positions. Each person has a slightly different angle at which the paper is most aligned with their bodies. Experiment with changing the angle of the paper in relation to your body so that you are comfortable. Remind yourself to take breaks every twenty minutes to stretch or move around the room. Search for the perfect writing tool for your needs, remembering that the width and weight of writing tools can vary greatly. Most people prefer a light, wider utensil to avoid gripping. Choose pens and pencils that make marks easily. There are special pens and pencils available that rest on top of the hand and prevent gripping with the thumb. As you begin to write, notice the two aspects of work required for handwriting: the effort it takes to hold the utensil and the work it takes to make a mark on the page. Avoid gripping and pressing, as this is too much effort for the task! If the lines on the page confine you, use a blank piece of paper and write as large and/or slanted as you wish. You will probably be the only one reading your notes, so the neatness once required in grade school is less important now. It is helpful to think of writing as drawing, allowing your hand and arm to follow through with movements initiated by the fingers. Humeroscapular rhythm is just as important in handwriting as it is in playing the piano! Notice the quality of the fingers in your writing hand, and try to maintain a neutral hand free of unnecessary flexion or extension. Be sure that you are not pressing too hard against the writing surface with your arm or planting your wrist on the page and making small repetitive movements against this fixture.

A mind map format is a helpful tool to integrate whole arm movements into your writing. The mind map records information similar to the way your brain works—utilizing a central concept with threads arising from it. Figure 3.1 in Chapter 3 (Inclusive Awareness) is an example of a mind map. To create a mind map, use a blank piece of paper and place your topic in the middle of the page surrounded by a circle. As ideas occur related to the topic, draw lines from the circle going outward and record your thoughts. Less is more in terms of verbiage—you need only to record the important phrases. Using colors can enhance the artistry of these mind maps and helps the handwriting incorporate the larger strokes of drawing. Finally, notice what happens to your writing when you are in a hurry. As with most tasks we hurry through, self-awareness diminishes the more we focus on the end rather than the means. Whenever possible, allow more time for handwriting so that you can keep awareness of your body using your kinesthetic sense.

Most of us use the computer on a daily basis, and we have certain habits and associations with this tool. To avoid injury at the computer, it may be necessary to make some adjustments to your daily routine. Begin by examining your work area. Is the chair adjustable, and is the desk at the height of best mechanical advantage? As we discovered at the piano, this would be where your forearms are parallel to the floor. Sit at balance with your head resting on the top cervical vertebrae, and notice how far you need to tilt your head down to see the screen. Most screens are adjustable so you can tilt your screen to maintain a visual field that does not compromise your head balance. Many sore necks have been caused by a lack of head balance and a thrusting forward of the head and neck to see the screen. Varying the arrangement of your work area helps reduce the risk of repetitive stress injury. A laptop computer allows you to stand at a counter or sit on the couch or at your desk while typing. In each of these possible areas it is important to notice your relationship to the computer in terms of torso balance and arm height. You may need to place something under the computer while standing or sitting on the couch to bring your arms parallel to the keys.

If you have been trained to maintain a basic home position at the computer keyboard, examine if twisting at the wrist is a movement you are frequently choosing in order to maintain this position. Twisting at the wrist can cause wrist pain, as this movement compresses the carpal (wrist) bones and impinges nerves, blood vessels, and tendons that run through the carpal tunnel. You may need to modify your typing to allow for more whole arm movements around the keyboard. A good exercise is to type with index fingers only to experience how much the whole arm can move as you type. You will need to look at your hands, of course, but this will allow a visual check for unnecessary twisting. Another harmful habit at the computer is dipping of the wrists. Just like at the piano, you want to be aware of the space available in the three joints of the wrist. Chronic dipping of the wrists leads to damage of the structures in the carpal tunnel. Rest the fingertips and base of the palm lightly on the keyboard and avoid fixing your wrists against the computer as a contact point. Some people find a small washcloth rolled up under their wrist is a helpful reminder to keep the wrist long, open, and free.

When using a freestanding mouse, try incorporating forearm rotation for clicking. This movement unifies the fingers, wrist, and arm, reducing the risk of finger isolation or twisting of the wrist. Be sure to listen to the sound of your typing. Are you banging away, using more effort than is needed to depress those shallow computer keys? Take a break every twenty minutes and stretch, checking in with your neck to be sure you are not gathering tension in this powerful area that governs the quality of the muscles in the rest of the body. As with handwriting, allow more time than you have previously to complete a task at the computer. To receive information from your kinesthetic sense about the nature and quality of your movements, you must slow down and allow time for feedback from the sensory neurons.

Chapter 26
Hearing Loss Prevention for Pianists

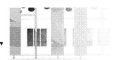

Many pianists listen to music in practice, performances, rehearsals, and lessons up to eight hours a day. Our auditory sense is vital to our well-being as musicians, and it should be understood and protected. Most classical musicians feel immune to the dangers of hearing loss from their profession, yet studies show that up to 52 percent of classical musicians and only about 30 percent of rock musicians suffer from hearing loss (as reported by Marshall Chasin in his very helpful book *Hear the Music*). By learning about the anatomy of the ear and the principles of sound conduction, we can incorporate this knowledge with measures to reduce the risk of hearing loss.

The human ear is divided into three sections: the outer, middle, and inner ear. The pinna on the outside and the eardrum on the inside define the outer ear. It includes the auditory canal. One of the functions of the outer ear is to amplify high frequencies (or pitches). It also creates resonance in the 3000 Hz range. Hertz (Hz) are defined as units of frequency or pitch. Middle C is 262 Hz, while the top note on the piano keyboard is just over 4000 Hz.

The middle ear consists of the eardrum and three tiny bones named the malleus (hammer), incus (anvil), and stapes (stirrup) for their respective shapes. These tiny bones transmit the sound waves from the eardrum (tympanic membrane) to the inner ear. One of the special qualities of the middle ear is impedance matching. This term refers to the matching of characteristics of the air in the ear canal to the fluid in the inner ear. Ninety-nine percent of energy is lost when sounds pass through an air-fluid barrier. Thus, the middle ear compensates for possible loss of sound. Another important characteristic of the middle ear is pressure release through the Eustachian tube that connects the back of the throat to the bottom of the middle ear. The middle ear also contains a muscular reflex that protects our hearing. The stapedius muscle, which is connected to the stapes bone, contracts in response to high intensity sound. It lessens the intensity of our voices, especially in the mid- and low-frequency sounds.

The inner ear, or cochlea, is a fluid-filled, snail-shaped structure about the size of the small fingernail. The basilar membrane, which covers the length of the spiral-shaped interior, contains tiny hair cells that transmit sound frequencies. The majority of these hair cells are connected to nerve fibers that send sensory signals to the brain or receive electrical impulses from the brain.

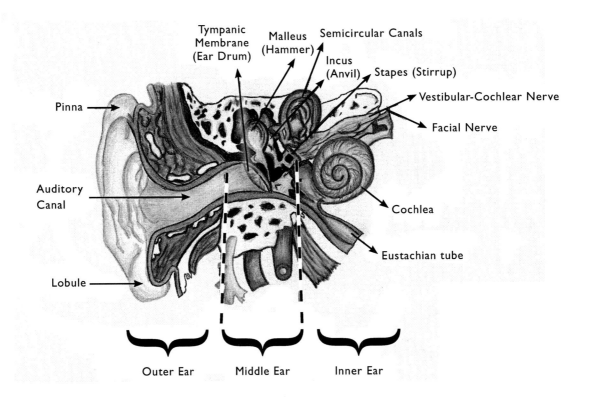

Figure 26.1. Parts of the Ear.

This delicate and complicated structure called the human ear is often taken for granted by musicians. We don't think about hearing loss until our ears are ringing—an early sign of hearing damage. If this occurs, remove any unnecessary sound from your environment for a period of twenty-four hours and the ringing will usually go away. It is best to avoid situations that might cause ringing in the ears by reducing the amount and intensity of sound exposure.

A special relationship between intensity, or decibel level, and time exposure described by Dr. Chasin in his book can help us make decisions about our environment that will reduce the risk of hearing loss. Decibels (dB) are defined as units of measurement pertaining to intensity or loudness of sound. If we can reduce the sound level by 3 dB, we can double our time exposure. Thus, music exposure for twenty hours per week at 88 dB would equal 85 dB for forty hours per week. This is good news for pianists who play and teach at least forty hours per week. By implementing measures to reduce the sound by a small amount, we can protect our ears. Pianists can practice with the lid down or on the small stick, except just before a concert when a fuller sound may be desired. Teachers can keep the lid down in their studios and sit away from the piano when it is being played. Creating distance between the sound source and the human ear reduces the decibel level. Lastly, you might consider investing in earplugs designed to reduce the decibel level across the frequency or pitch range. This full spectrum sound reduction assures that the sound is not muted or distorted. The ER20XS is an earplug that serves this purpose and is available online for a reasonable price. A reduction of 20 dB across the pitch spectrum is provided by the ER20XS.

If you attend concerts where the sound is louder than is comfortable for your ears, bring along these earplugs. Indoor venues often create decibel levels that are harmful. Whether it is a rock or symphonic venue, potential for hearing damage exists. Be sure to educate your young students about the hazards of attending concerts where the sound is unnecessarily loud. Unfortunately, this problem exists in most venues for popular music, and many bands pride themselves on their ear-splitting sound systems. It is important that we take the protection of hearing into account when we perform. Some concert halls are small, and a very large piano played at full volume with the lid on the long stick may be too much for the audience. Be proactive in your choices for your studio and concerts to promote awareness of the need to protect the auditory sense.

Chapter 27
Recovering from Injury

Injury among musicians is a very common problem. Studies vary, but an average of several shows that 40 to 60 percent of musicians suffer from pain or injury at some point that affects their musical careers. It is difficult to document musicians' injuries, as there is no benefit, and often harm, in reporting a problem. Accompanists have been replaced, graduate teaching assistants have lost their positions, and pianists have been encouraged to find another career after admitting to an injury. However, through knowledge, self-care, retraining of movements, and appropriate medical intervention, most musicians can recover from injury and resume successful careers.

The first step to recovery involves determining what structures the injury involves. This may require a medical diagnosis. It is usually a good idea to see a physician experienced in working with musicians, if possible, as our problems are unique. A physician may prescribe medications and treatment, but often you can alleviate the symptoms with home remedies and over-the-counter anti-inflammatory agents. The most common diagnoses for injury among pianists are tendonitis, carpal tunnel syndrome, and thoracic outlet syndrome.

Tendonitis is the inflammation of a tendon and commonly occurs in the forearm, elbow, and shoulder regions. Often this occurs when the affected area has been overused or misused. Tendons are part of the connective tissue system of our bodies, and they arise from the fascia, or covering, of the muscle to become rope-like structures that attach muscle to bone. When these structures become inflamed, the area becomes painful and difficult to move easily. Alternating heat and cold to the painful region can reduce swelling and pain. The most recent studies regarding hot and cold treatment recommend alternation at short intervals with moderate temperatures in each extreme. One way to achieve this would be to apply an ice pack with a towel beneath it alternating with a heating pad on medium temperature for a few minutes each. Alternating heat and cold is most helpful in the acute phase of inflammation; after five to seven days use only heat. Over-the-counter anti-inflammatory agents such as ibuprofen will alleviate the symptoms for a period of time. They should not be used for longer than a few weeks, as liver or kidney damage is a serious side effect. Many injured pianists have found relief through the dietary supplement MSM (methylsulfonylmethane). Dr. Stanley Jacobs at the Oregon Health Sciences University studied this dietary supplement for its anti-inflammatory properties. His book *The Miracle of MSM* (1999) documents his clinical studies and findings. Unlike ibuprofen, MSM has no significant long-term side effects. Physical therapy can also alleviate the symptoms of tendonitis. Understanding the structure and function of joints related to the inflamed area and retraining of movements are essential to the healing process.

Carpal tunnel syndrome is another common injury reported by pianists. It refers to a combination of symptoms that occur when the median nerve is compressed in the carpal tunnel. These symptoms include numbness and tingling in the thumb, index, and long fingers, and wrist pain. Usually this problem is caused by unnecessary compression of the bones of the wrist due to excessive wrist dropping or twisting. Both of these movements cause the wrist bones to scrunch together, compressing vital structures passing through the carpal tunnel. Hot and cold therapy, anti-inflammatories, and physical therapy can help this condition. The single most important factor in recovering from carpal tunnel syndrome is an understanding of the structure and function of the wrist joints.

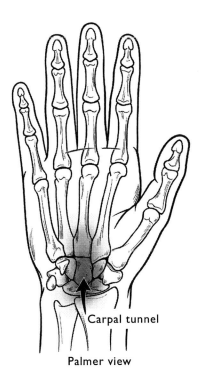

Carpal tunnel

Palmer view

Figure 27.1. Bones of the Right Hand and Wrist.

Thoracic outlet syndrome also occurs at an alarming rate among pianists. This term refers to a group of distinct disorders that affect the nerves in the brachial plexus and the nerves and blood vessels between the base of the neck and underarm. Symptoms include pain, numbness, tingling, and weakness. The vital structures in the region associated with thoracic outlet syndrome are very often compressed by an arm structure that is habitually carried in the lowest position. When the arm structure is pulled down, nerves and blood vessels arising from the brachial plexus are compressed by the collarbone, which they travel beneath. Understanding the suspension of the arm structure and regaining its buoyant relationship to the underlying structures will alleviate this compression. Often physical therapy or massage is required to coax the muscles and connective tissue of the upper torso back to a place where the arm structure is floating above the ribs. Movement retraining includes a keen awareness of humeroscapular rhythm and whole arm movements for all activities.

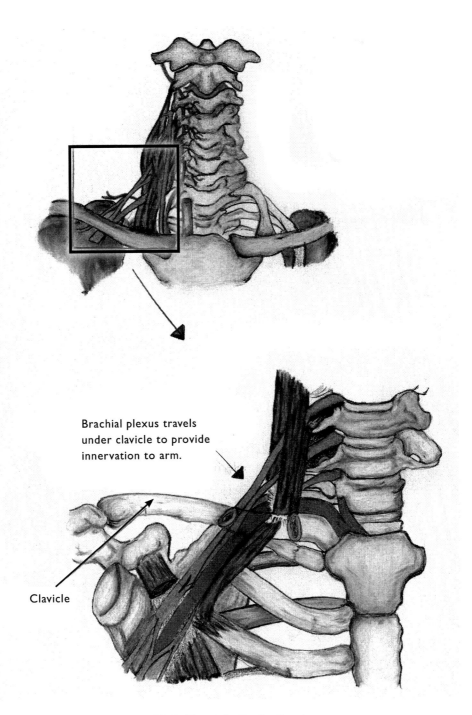

Brachial plexus travels
under clavicle to provide
innervation to arm.

Clavicle

Figure 27.2. Thoracic Outlet Syndrome.

It is important that you develop a healthy practice routine that includes awareness and excellent body use. Be aware of the temperature of your body and in your practice space. Practicing in a cold environment or with a cold body can lead to injury. Use warm water, a heating pad, or aerobic exercise to warm your body, and consider using a space heater, as appropriate, in your practice area. Evaluate the condition of your instrument, including the key weight as described in Chapter 9, and the resistance of the pedals. It is important to have your piano tuned and regulated frequently. As you begin to practice, keep in mind this quote from Will Durant: "We are what we repeatedly do. Excellence, then, is not an act but a habit."[10] Our state of being in the practice room is the presence we bring to the performance. Maintaining a calm, centered awareness inclusive of all aspects of music making as outlined in Chapter 3 is essential. Use awareness of your breathing before and during practicing to keep you relaxed and present in the moment. Be sure to warm up for eight to ten minutes with slow scales, improvisation, or easy pieces. The brain and body need ample time to prepare for the complicated task of music making. Once you begin to practice, take a break every twenty to thirty minutes to stretch, walk around, or get some water.

Whatever the source or nature of the injury, patience and persistence are key elements to the recovery process. Most pianists play without self-awareness and with poor movements for many years before injury ensues. It will take some time to retrain your body to use the most efficient, tension-free movements necessary to recover and reduce the risk of re-injury. Having a trained teacher is essential for this process. Although you can read about movement retraining, understanding it will require the sensory experience of the new, correct movements. These new habits of movement are best guided by a trained teacher who understands the structure and function of the body as it relates to playing the piano.

If you are injured, make it your mission to amplify your self-awareness and self-care. Notice what daily activities aggravate your pain, and change or reduce them.

---

10. Will Durant, *The Story of Philosophy: The Lives and Opinions of the Greater Philosophers*, 2nd ed. (Garden City, NY: Garden City Publishing, 1933), 87.

If you cannot garden without aggravating your tendonitis, get some help until you have figured out how to complete this activity without pain. Be holistic in your quest for health, addressing all aspects of your well-being, including diet, sleep, and exercise. Most of us could improve our diets with a few simple modifications, such as reducing sugar or increasing fruits and vegetables. By increasing your sleep to eight or nine hours a night (the National Sleep Foundation's recommendation for adults over twenty-one years of age), you will give your body a chance to rest and repair. When designing an exercise plan, keep in mind that gentle stretching of the muscles and connective tissue is a great way to regain flexibility. The injured part will recover much more quickly if the whole of you is healthy and strong.

Realize that you are not alone as an injured pianist and you have not knowingly done anything wrong. Remember that statistics show 40 to 60 percent of musicians suffer from injury. With the advent of somatic music education (music education that educates musicians about the structure and function of their bodies), this epidemic trend can be reversed. Often the path to recovery yields new discoveries about techniques and artistry that you might not have previously realized. By increasing the awareness of your body and retraining your movements, you will simultaneously become a teacher fully equipped to help your students avoid the risk of injury.

Bibliography

Alexander, F. M. *The Use of the Self*. London: Orion, 2001.

Benson, Herbert. *The Relaxation Response*. New York: HarperCollins, 2000.

Conable, Barbara. *How to Learn the Alexander Technique*. Portland: Andover Press, 1991.

Conable, Barbara. *The Structures and Movement of Breathing*. Chicago: GIA Publications, Inc., 2000.

Conable, Barbara. *What Every Musician Needs to Know About the Body*. Portland: Andover Press, 1998.

Chasin, Marshall. *Hear the Music: A Guide to Hearing Loss Prevention*. 6th ed. Toronto: Chasin, 2019.

Gerig, Reginald. *Famous Pianists and Their Techniques*. 2nd ed. Bloomington: Indiana University Press, 1974.

Jacob, Stanley W. *The Miracle of MSM: The Natural Solution for Pain*. New York: Medusa, 1995.

Mark, Thomas. *What Every Pianist Needs to Know About the Body*. Chicago: GIA Publications, Inc., 2003.

Matthay, Tobias. *The Act of Touch in All Its Diversity*. London: Bosworth & Co. Ltd., 1903.

Matthay, Tobias. *The Visible and Invisible in Piano Technique*. London: Oxford University Press, 1977.

McCracken, Thomas O., ed. *The New Atlas of Human Anatomy*. New York: MetroBooks, 2000.

Ortmann, Otto. *The Physical Basis of Piano Touch and Tone.* New York: E. P. Dutton & Co., 1925.

Philip, Robert. *Performing Music in the Age of Recording.* New Haven: Yale University Press, 2004.

The Taubman Techniques. VHS. Directed by Ernest Urvater. Medusa, NY: The Taubman Institute, 1995, 2001.

About the Author

Lisa Marsh is Director of the Coordinate Movement Program at Portland State University, where she specializes in wellness for musicians and retraining injured musicians. Her courses focus on injury prevention, health and well-being for musicians, and mind-body connections for increased artistry and creativity. She received her Bachelor of Science in Music and Master of Music in Performance from Portland State University. Additional background experience includes nineteen years as a registered nurse in the fields of Neurosurgery and Emergency Medicine, eight years of piano technique study at the Taubman Institute of Piano, and fifteen years of study of the Alexander Technique and Body Mapping with Barbara Conable. Ms. Marsh is a certified Andover Educator and Sponsoring Teacher for licensure in Body Mapping.

Lisa Marsh is former Principle Keyboard with the Columbia Symphony Orchestra and pianist with the Marsh-Titterington Piano Duo. Her original compositions reflect diverse influences and are often inspired by her environment and the artists she collaborates with.

www.coordinatemovement.com

www.LisaAnnMarsh.com